EVERY WAKING
MOMENT

Training for the Ultimate Karate Test

Goran Powell

Foreword by Gavin Mulholland

EVERY WAKING MOMENT
ISBN: 1523812060
ISBN-13: 978-1523812066

By the same author:

Non-fiction
Waking Dragons

Fiction
A Sudden Dawn
Chojun
Matryoshka

To the martial artists who put their trust in me,
shared their fears, and their triumphs.

Contents

APPENDIX 1

APPENDIX 2

Foreword

On 15 December 2002, I watched as Goran Powell stepped out from behind the shoji screen and onto the balcony overlooking the training area of the Meidokan dojo in Kilburn, north London.

He was there to face a waiting line of thirty fighters. The line was so long, it stretched fully around three sides of the dojo. With a greater number of people along to watch and support, the place was packed with close to a hundred excited and nervous people, yet eerily, the room was in complete silence as all eyes turned to watch as Goran emerged to face the test.

After months of hardship and gruelling preparation his time had come. He was about to face the awesome Thirty Man Kumite, a legendary event in karate circles where one man fights thirty men. Thirty fights, full contact, one minute rounds, a fresh fighter every round. Nowhere to run. Nowhere to hide.

I watched as he made his way to the top of the stairs where he paused – and I saw the blood drain from his face as he looked down on the line of fighters that had turned up specifically for this fight.

I saw him get control, steel himself and, as quickly as it came, the moment passed. He walked down the stairs confidently, even nodding greetings to some of the fighters that had travelled a long way to do him the honour of being part of his ultimate test.

On command, the fighters snapped to attention. I put my

hands on Goran's shoulders and looked deep into his eyes, deep into his soul, a soul that would soon be stripped bare for all to see. He was looking back, but not really seeing. It was a look I had seen many times before, and have seen many times since – but only ever in the eyes of those who have made huge sacrifices and gone through serious hardship – a look sometimes known as *The Thousand Yard Stare*. And he had it.

'Ready?' I asked, though I already knew the answer. *'Osu,'* came the simple reply. And without any further ceremony, the first fighter stepped out and the test began.

Since that time – he survived the test, by the way – Goran has taken a key role in the preparation of other young (and not-so-young) karate-ka, seeking to find their own ultimate-truth and discover who they really are through the furnace that is the Thirty Man Kumite.

Goran, a writer by trade, wrote eloquently about his own experience of the test in his best-selling book *'Waking Dragons'* but now, more than ten years on, he approaches the experience from a very different point of view – that of a teacher, a coach, a sensei.

To achieve the levels of fitness, grit and skill required to prevail in the Thirty Man Kumite requires a high degree of self-focus, selfishness even, as the task ahead becomes all-consuming and every waking moment is taken up with training for, dreading, thinking about, fearing and getting ready for the test.

In this truly remarkable book, Goran pays everything back. Turning that self-focus, that fear, that dread and all

7

that training, outward to the benefit of others. Here he not only talks about the Thirty Man, he lays out how to face it, how to prepare for it and ultimately, how to pass it.

I know of no other test that pushes people as far as the Thirty Man Kumite and I know of no other book that can prepare you to face such a test quite like this one.

The meaning of the word *'Sensei'* is not really *'teacher'* as many people assume, but more literally *'one who has gone before'* and in this book, you have the opportunity to learn from one who has faced the line and prevailed, one who has analysed the myriad of lessons it had to offer and come out with a logical, structured and most importantly, achievable plan on how to get through it.

One who has gone before... Sensei Goran Powell.

Shihan Gavin Mulholland (6th Dan)
Chief Instructor, London
Daigaku Karate Kai

A Field, Revisited

The shadows are getting longer but at this time of year there's still plenty of light. It's late afternoon, mid-June, on the second day of summer camp. We've already had six hours of hard training but there's one more event before we finish for the day. It's short compared to a lesson, or even the most novice grading, but of such fierce intensity that it can sometimes seem to go on forever.

Sensei Gavin has instructed all green belts and higher to assemble on The Field of Truth in fifteen minutes. The first time he did this, at summer camp 2000, no one had known what to expect. But now it's 2006 and there's no uncertainty. The happy buzz of the team games is quickly replaced by a more serious mood. Even the air temperature seems to drop by a few degrees. We will be fighting soon. One of our number, Dominic Du Plooy, is about to take the final part of his nidan (2nd dan) grading – the Thirty Man Kumite. He must complete thirty full-contact fights with only a two minute break after ten fights and twenty fights.

I make my way through the long grass to my tent. Getting ready for this event has become something of a ritual for me. First, I don my groin box and give it a couple of taps to make sure nothing's tangled up in the wrong place. Next, I tie my trousers and wrap my gi around my waist. My fingers secure my belt with movement made familiar from years of repetition and pull it tight with two firm tugs. I refill my water bottle and check my gum-shield is in my bag. I add a raincoat, just in case. The weather can turn easily at this time of year.

When I arrive on the Field of Truth, a line of people is combing the grass like a police search, clearing the ground of stones and branches. A table and chair has been set up for the timekeeper and a row of spectators has formed across the top of the field. Some are karate-ka who aren't fighting today and the rest are friends and family. On the bottom end, a line of fighters has begun forming beneath the tall overhanging trees. There's some confusion at the far end about who's in and who's out. Sensei Gavin counts and recounts until thirty fighters are firmly in place. At my end there's no confusion. We've all been here before and we know we'll be fighting.

Standing opposite, alone with his thoughts, is Dom. Beneath the brim of his sun-hat, his eyes are staring into the middle distance. He's moving his limbs lightly to ease the adrenaline racing through his body to prepare him for what lies ahead. He looks to be handling the nerves well. I'm glad, because it's a nervous moment for me too. I've been working with him for several months to help him prepare and today we'll see the result of our efforts.

I feel the training has gone well. Dom was always technically good, fast, accurate, fit and determined. Better still, he's picked up every drill and built his fitness to an impressive peak. But Dom is one of our smallest and lightest fighters and we are thirty big strong guys. We both know that no amount of cardio will keep him dancing out of trouble for thirty rounds. Eventually he'll get hit, and hit hard. And ironically, the last person doing that, when he's at his most tired, will be me.

As usual there's little ceremony or preamble. Dom bows to the chief instructors, and the line, and the first fighter is called out. Dom begins a little stiffly. The nerves are freezing his limbs and he's not moving as smoothly as I'd like. He's clashing instead of blending, miss-timing his blocks and punches.

However by the third fight he's warming to the task and moving more fluently. We've been working on hitting and moving – the key to success in this test – and now he's doing just that. Being light on his feet, he's moving in and out just like we practised. I shout my encouragement, 'Just like that, Dom!' although I doubt he can hear me at the far end of the field.

The test goes on with ruthless efficiency. One minute of hard fighting, a few seconds of rest during the changeover, a quick bow, and it begins again. This relentless rhythm takes Dom to his tenth fight where he gets a two minute break. I'm pleased to see our training is working. He looks tired but in control, sipping water and steeling himself for what's coming next.

From my own experience I can recall the feeling of hitting a wall somewhere around fight six or seven. This is where you're no longer fighting fresh and your limbs begin to weigh heavy. However most fighters agree it's somewhere in the middle ten fights that a deep tiredness sets in. There's no dancing now. Footwork has gone from a spring and a skip to plodding steps. Each fight is another gruelling trip to the trenches.

Dom is tiring but he's still doing everything right, hitting and moving, switching stance and firing back. He's looking focused and staying in the game. But as he approaches twenty fights, he comes up against two of the biggest and most ferocious strikers in the association. One is Neil Grove, 6'6" and 20 stone, who went on to an international career in cage fighting that took him all the way to the UFC. The other is Dave Urquhart, 6'5" and 15 stone, who has dominated the kumite division at DKK tournaments for the last few years. To make matters worse, fights nineteen and twenty are some of the most testing of all. You're coming to the end of twenty minutes of hard fighting with no finish in sight. It's too early to kick for home. All you can do is hold on and try and make it to the way-station of twenty fights and a brief respite.

Neil is fighting with good control but I know from experience his punches feel like being hit by a battering ram. He's putting Dom under unrelenting pressure. Dom weathers the storm only to face Dave for his twentieth fight. I'm watching and Dave seems to tower over Dom by at least a foot. Dave fires his shots with ferocious accuracy and Dom looks to be taking heavy punishment. Dave is relentless and aggressive, throwing combinations so fast it's hard to know what's happening. Dom's in the grip of a violent storm. Pale, soaked in sweat, bleeding from the nose, fighting to survive. This is no longer a question of skill or conditioning. All that's keeping him standing right now is raw courage, bubbling up from somewhere deep inside. I feel helpless. This wasn't something we could have replicated in training. Only the test itself can bring forth this kind of pressure. This was what I'd worried about. This was the moment of truth.

I'd been concerned Dom was too small for such a line-up. I'd concentrated on building fitness, technique, strategy, tactics, mind-set – and we'd done all that. Yet still I'd harboured doubts and fears. But watching him now, fighting on will and desire, I feel a pang of guilt for doubting him. All of a sudden, I'm so moved by what I'm seeing that I'm forced to turn away. And strangely, despite the mayhem of the fighting and the roar of the crowd, Sensei Gavin notices and asks if I'm alright. I reassure him I'm fine – just a touch of hay-fever troubling my eyes.

Ten minutes later my sweat-soaked, blood-stained protégé is standing before me for his final fight. Gavin calls 'Hajime' and the crowd yells loud encouragement. Dom is still kicking and punching. He's weathering the hooks I'm slamming into his ribs and the low kicks across his thighs. No fancy footwork now, he's standing and trading. He's elevated above the pain I know he must be feeling. Then Gavin is shouting something, but I can't hear above the din. Are we done?

'Ten seconds more!'

We close again. Gasping, flailing, eating up the blows, Dom isn't letting up. Finally Gavin barges between us to end the fight. Time must have been called but I hadn't heard. Dom's gi is hanging open and he's swaying with tiredness and emotion as we bow.

A minute later, once the formalities of the line have been observed, I hurry to embrace him.

'Sorry I wasn't cold,' he mutters in my ear.

It takes me a moment to understand what he's talking about. 'Cold' was a concept we'd developed in our training. When you're trying to generate ferocity you can get a bit blinded by your own aggression. The Red Mist descends and it can cloud your vision. So I'd encouraged Dom to imagine turning a red heat to blue and feeling 'cold' about the hurt he was inflicting. It was a visualisation technique that had worked well and given him more focus. But in that final minute, with the end in sight, there'd been far too much emotion to be cold.

'Forget it,' I laugh, gripping his shoulders. 'You did everything just right, and more.'

A few weeks later we went for a curry to celebrate our journey together. I mentioned how emotional I'd felt when he'd looked to be on his last legs against Dave Urquhart. To my surprise, Dom didn't remember it the same way. He said he'd felt fine and had considered it just another fight. I recalled a similar feeling in my own test a few years earlier. Against the hardest fighters, and at my most tired, my mind had been calm and focused. My body had moved naturally. My spirit had been serene. Well almost. If ever I've experienced a Zen moment in my karate, that was it.

In my book about my test, Waking Dragons (available from all good booksellers) I likened this inner calm to a pilot light, a flame burning inside you that no one can reach in and extinguish – except you. This description resonated with a great many martial artists who experienced similar focus in the deepest adversity. I tried to make it clear in that book, as in this one, that the dragons of the title are not the fighters in the line, or those facing the line. They are the fears and dreads that lie coiled deep inside each of us. Through a long programme of training and development, and an epic test at the end, these fears can be faced. Like dragons, they can be woken and they can be slain.

Since my own Thirty Man Kumite I have gone on to coach many more fighters and offer advice to plenty more. Generally my fighters have acquitted themselves well. That's not to say others haven't – many did, and there have been plenty of memorable performances without my help. However from coaching, and participating as the final fighter in the line, I've come to know this test more intimately than most.

As is so often the case in martial arts, I've learnt from teaching. I've coached fighters who were fit and unfit, technical and scrappy, big and small, male and female. Age and injuries have played a part and we've learnt to work around them. One of the most impressive line-ups of recent years was completed by Juha Makinen at the age of forty-six. I've shared in the training, the nerves, the test and the reward, and I've felt privileged to have done so. If you find yourself facing a similar test, or you're coaching a fighter in such a venture, I'm happy to share what I've learnt with you.

The Ultimate Test

Step into the ring or the cage and you risk getting hurt. You might get knocked out. But you also have a fair chance of winning. If you've trained properly, you should be thinking positively and believe you're going to win. You could score a knockout in the first ten seconds and be celebrating with your corner moments later. If the fight goes the distance you'll get tired. But then so will your opponent. So you still have a decent chance of winning.

Only two of these are true in the Thirty Man Kumite:

You risk getting hurt.

And you could get knocked out.

You're never going to win. You won't look good, at least not for long. Each fighter will be fresher than you. Towards the end, they'll be better than you. You have a big punch? Big deal. You'll be lucky to land any sort of punch. Fast hands? They'll feel like lead weights. High kicks? Each one will sap your energy and risk a takedown. Great cardio? Try dancing on dead legs. You can take a shot? Well at least that'll come in handy...

The Thirty Man Kumite promises nothing but hardship. To get through in any sort of shape you're going to need every aspect of the stand-up fighter's game. That means skill, technique, ring-craft, strategy, tactics, cardio, conditioning. Above all, you'll need the mental strength to hold your focus when it feels like all hell is breaking loose around you.

It's for this reason that the Thirty Man Kumite has become such a milestone in the DKK system. Previous tests have been quite general. The shodan (1st dan) grading begins with a long fitness test – ironically called a 'warm-up' – and goes on to cover kihon, kata, bunkai, pad-work, conditioning, weapons, multiples, sparring, grappling and breaking. It rumbles on for over 4 hours and by the end there's no doubt you can perform strongly under intense pressure. However the word 'shodan' means 'beginner's level' and it suggests the black belt, while certainly no longer a novice, is finally ready to take the first step on the road to mastery.

In DKK the nidan (2nd dan) test is the first step on this road. It is a specialist grading, and that specialism is kumite (sparring). It's a chance to delve deeply into every aspect of the stand-up fighter's game and, in theory, it takes place when the candidate is at his or her physical peak, around the age of thirty. While there's a new kata to learn, and some private Q&A with instructors, the main focus is the Thirty Man line-up.

Instead of casting the net wide, the nidan candidate must go deep. The criteria for the test are starkly simple: kicking and punching for thirty minutes. But every kick and punch, every block and parry has to be hard enough to carry you through thirty punishing rounds. The spectre of hurt and failure hangs over you from the start, so if ever there's a time to seek perfection, this is it. And like so often in karate, perfection begins by getting the fundamentals absolutely right.

Paradoxically, the road to advancement begins by going back to basics. This concept of digging deeper into what we already know – or think we know – is repeated in subsequent gradings. Third dan is an instructor's grade where candidates must teach basics to beginners. Teaching others demands a far deeper understanding of a subject than simply knowing it yourself. Fourth dan is a weapons grading where the candidate must develop skills in kobudo and knife defence, and tie these skills back into empty-handed fighting. However while these tests may be more elevated than the nidan grading, the personal stakes are never higher than for the candidate facing the Thirty Man Kumite.

Finally, on the subject of the Thirty Man Kumite, I should make it clear that plenty of female fighters from DKK have tested themselves against female line-ups and acquitted themselves with honour. However calling it the 'Thirty Woman Kumite' just doesn't sound right. The Thirty Man Kumite, like the Fifty and Hundred Man Kumite, is the title of a test that's renowned in the martial arts world and carries equal kudos for men and women. Similarly I refer to fighters as 'he' rather than 'he or she', or 'they', for brevity and clarity, no disrespect intended. I'm in accordance with Sensei Gavin in finding the women of DKK inspirational. They fight bigger, heavier opponents in every class, which means they train harder, show more courage (and often better technique) than many of the guys. Several women who completed the test recently were also mums with young children and finding the time to prepare must have been a challenge in itself. In fact, maybe the Thirty Woman Kumite should be known as the ultimate test, after all?

The Total Fighter

When a candidate comes to me for coaching, our first session is a form of health-check. In my head I hold a blueprint of what I call the Total Fighter and I check the candidate against it. Just to be clear, this is a stand-up fighter – while Goju Ryu karate contains grappling, there's no ground-fighting in the Thirty Man.

My blueprint resembles a pyramid with three levels. The bottom level is the foundation of a good fighter and relates to footwork and body movement. In karate this would come under stance-work. I'm looking at the fighter's ability to hit a basic position like zenkutsu dachi with power and precision while on the move. However, as I hope you know, these stances are positions frozen in time and only half the story. The other half is the ability to move freely in a fighting stance and hit these positions at will. In short, the foundation of the Total Fighter is the ability to hit and move.

Fifteen years as the final fight in the Thirty Man Kumite

has proved this to me beyond all doubt. The fighters who finished strongly were active and mobile. Static fighters soaked up a lot more punishment. By the time they got to me, their bodies and limbs were deadened by repeated blows. Sadly for them, that meant they had to take even more.

While size should matter – and it does – movement matters more. Some of the strongest finishers were smaller guys who, through great cardio and footwork, moved through thirty bouts and fought strongly to the very end. The rule applies equally for big guys. The ones who moved well finished strongly. The ones who didn't took more punishment.

However while striking on the move is fundamental, no fighter can expect to dance away from everything. So the middle section of the pyramid relates to moving correctly inside striking range. Here I look at both offensive and defensive skills. Offensively, we look at the striking power of the left and right hand (front-punch, reverse, hook and uppercut) and the left and right leg (front, round and low kick). I'm not interested in fancy kicks or tricksy combinations at this stage. They are nice to have once the fundamentals are in place.

Defensively, I look at reaction speed against punches, front kicks, round kicks and low kicks. This is important because when you're tired – which is most of the time – your opponent will initiate and you must react. That means whether or not you're a natural counter-puncher, you need to develop this skill for this test.

While the first two levels of the pyramid are physical movements based on strategy (hit and move) and tactics (striking and reacting) I reserve the top of the pyramid for mind-set. Put another way, levels one and two are elements of mind and body while level three is spirit. In spirit I include far more than simply fighting spirit. This is the maturity needed to set a punishing regime and stick to it. The emotional intelligence to negotiate with partners to spend extra time on karate. The quiet determination to overcome setbacks and work around injuries. These are the unseen battles of the Thirty Man Kumite and in truth, this is where pass or fail is decided.

After testing the nidan candidate against the blueprint, my first interest is correcting imbalances. For example, powerful strikes but poor ring-craft, or a big right hand but a weak left. The aim is to create a fighter with no obvious weaknesses. This attention to areas of weakness is vital because good fighters attack the weak points, and the line-up is full of good fighters. Like sharks scenting blood, they'll sniff out weakness and home in on it. So the first thing to work on is plugging the gaps in the fighter's game.

If the weakness is technical, we spend time building correct technique. This often means going back to fundamentals and using kihon-ido (moving basics) to see where the problem lies. Because kihon-ido is so prescriptive, it helps me to see what's wrong. I can usually spot small errors that tell me where to direct our training. Is the stance long and stable? Is there full loading in the hips and shoulders? Is the breathing too soft or too tense? Are the strikes off-target? Does the gaze seem to be drifting left or right? It's important to fix any or all of these early on. I recommend at least five minutes of kihon a day if you're good – and fifteen minutes if you're not – to keep the fundamentals primed. After all, these are essential for range, power, energy and kime (focus) and the benefits feed into your other training once the pressure gets dialled up.

If the imbalance is physical, we might do fitness, although at this stage I expect the fighter to be building fitness in his own time. If the weakness is a low fighting spirit, perhaps through lack of confidence, I park this for a while. Confidence is something we will build later, based on solid foundations and hard training. In the meantime fear is a good motivator.

The Coach

It's important to understand the difference between a coach and a sensei. The sensei is responsible for the whole club, not just one student. He's putting a hard test before the nidan candidate and judging pass or fail without bias. While he wants the candidate to succeed, he must remain impartial. He has the association's interests at heart and, as Sensei Gavin frequently reminds us, failure is good to keep the standards high.

The coach, on the other hand, can and should always have

the candidate's best interests at heart. So if there's one piece of advice I can give you about coaching, it's to work towards success, not failure. That means setting achievable goals for every session so your fighter never feels he's failed. The idea of 'working to failure' is a common one in fitness. It means doing reps until you can't do another. While it might work for bodybuilders, it's not right for fighters. A bodybuilder can do squats 'to failure' because he's probably doing a split routine and won't train his legs again for several days. That's not the same with a fighter, who needs to use his legs again the next day. Instead, work towards building good form and holding it as long as possible. By all means get intense and ferocious, but when your fighter begins to tighten up and lose form, switch to a new exercise. Build a 'rolling' mind-set that doesn't grind away at things that aren't working. Learn to switch and change, just like a fight does. This way you get used to quality and success.

As a coach, you must be clear about where your fighter needs to improve most. Set him simple, memorable exercises, to be done in his own time, and expect him to be a bit better each time you see him. Urge him stick to your programme and discourage others from offering advice, especially if it's conflicting. If others want to help, they can do fitness and conditioning but that's all. Your fighter needs a clear strategy to focus on – make sure it's yours.

Structure your training around dojo classes and complement them in your own programme. If dojo training is going through a hard physical phase, add a little more technical training. If dojo sessions are light, make things more demanding.

In the long build up to the test, aim to do every exercise and drill with good form. Form is a subtle thing that takes time to perfect. If your fighter is struggling, break the exercise down into more basic parts until he can do each bit right. Then reassemble. Once your fighter is training with good form, you can begin to push fitness and add exercises beyond fundamentals – high-kicks, clinch-work and more complex drills.

In the last eight weeks concentrate on 'holding form' under pressure. Ramp up the energy levels, switch on the mental focus and work until form goes. Then stop. That means the fighter is always training with high energy and good form. He doesn't get used to slogging and grinding. Rather than 'failing', he gets stopped while his performance is still relatively good. This way he recovers faster and gets back into quality training sooner.

If your fighter is following a five-day programme and working hard at least three of those days, you must appreciate his effort. Elevate your fighter by building on his success week by week. Most of the time, he should be self-motivated. The prospect of the Thirty Man is enough to get anyone working hard and I've yet to encounter a fighter who didn't. However there are times when you need to pick up flagging spirits or correct poor form and you do this with your voice. Your instructions, your tone and manner, can add an extra ten percent to every session if you get them right. But get them wrong and you can rob your fighter of confidence and energy. Remember you're building on success. Don't behave like a sergeant major with a raw recruit where nothing's good enough. Respect your fighter's efforts and work with what you've got. If his technique is good then let him practice and only pick up on obvious mistakes or flagging effort.

If you shout at him to hit harder, he should at least try and oblige. Men tend to rise to what they see as a challenge. Women sometimes react differently. Whoever you're training with, be aware of the responses you get and be prepared to adjust. It helps to frame your instruction as a challenge rather than a criticism. There's a big difference between being encouraged to hit harder and being told your punch is crap. Shouting words like 'rubbish' is childish and counterproductive. Too much perceived criticism will sap anyone's will and confidence. In contrast, 'harder' sets a goal for the fighter to aim for, something higher and better.

Most people respond well to praise. They get a buzz from knowing they're doing something right. You'll often get a surge in effort to keep the buzz going a little longer. Just occasionally a tired fighter will see praise as an excuse to slow down. If this is the case, make sure your praise is active and loud rather than quiet and reassuring. Or take away the praise and revert to commands.

The tone of your voice is important. Use a powerful voice full of energy and your fighter will be drawn along by it. Keep him going for one more round. If he's working hard, avoid stopping and nitpicking. Correct things one at a time, at the end of each round, to avoid an overload of negativity.

Each time you coach a new fighter, be prepared to experiment and adapt to find motivation that works. And remember women are strange chaps so they may not respond like guys. I learnt this the hard way with the very first fighter I coached, my fiancée at the time and now my darling wife, Charmaigne.

The Happy Couple

When Charmaigne asked me to help her to prepare for the Thirty Man Kumite, I'd completed my own test the year before. I knew what had worked for me and I was happy to share my wisdom with her. I felt she was a talented fighter but her style didn't suit her physique. She was medium height and quite strong, but light and willowy. Yet she would stand and trade with all comers. This showed good spirit but for a lighter fighter it was a poor strategy. The smaller fighter needs to use more body movement against bigger opponents, so I suggested she should adjust her style. Luckily this made sense to her and she agreed to try. Better still, she picked up my footwork and ring-craft drills quickly and soon made them her own.

But not everything was so easy. When I urged her to do morning sprints across the football pitch like I'd done, she was reluctant. Apparently she wasn't 'a morning person'. And she didn't like wet muddy grass. After a few tries, she simply stopped doing it. I insisted. She refused. Several days were spent regarding one another across the demilitarised zone, until she went to the gym at lunchtime and did thirty minutes on the treadmill. It wasn't what I'd done, but it was good enough and we were able to move on. There were more dark clouds looming.

After several weeks of getting her footwork in place it was time to dial up the intensity. When a fighter's hitting pads, I usually count to keep them on track. If their effort dips a little low, I tell them, 'Pick it up!' and this normally gets a renewed effort. I acknowledge this with something like, 'Lovely! And again! One more time!' to keep the positive energy flowing a little longer. This way I try and coax the best performance from them. I'm guided mostly by their efforts, but with little a touch of carrot and stick, when required.

This didn't work with Charmaigne. She responded well to the carrot but she didn't like the stick. Not one bit. If I shouted – or said anything that implied she wasn't doing enough – her performance would drop instead of rise. We discussed it and she felt this criticism was sapping her energy. When I shouted to try and drop her adrenaline, things got even worse.

I was reluctant to change. Not because I like shouting (although I do!) but because I felt it helped to recreate the noise and furore of the Thirty Man. You have to learn to perform under this kind of pressure. But Charmaigne wasn't having any of it and we were back to the DMZ.

I tried other ways to fire her up and in the end, we found being competitive worked best. We would take an imaginary opponent and Charmaigne would have to 'Be faster!' and 'Be better!' – I had to avoid 'hit harder!' because (again!) this didn't sit right with her. She didn't want to train with the intention of hurting another person, especially not a woman. That was fine with me because she was hitting the pad pretty damn hard anyway – so much so that I recall some reluctance among the ladies to spar with her at all.

This was an important lesson for me as a coach. The relationship between fighter and coach must be flexible. Perhaps the coach's most important skill is the ability to tailor the training to a fighter. Each fighter is different, so each regime should be too. The blueprint of the total fighter is a constant. Many of the exercises and drills are constant. The test itself is constant. However the emphasis should change with each fighter. Working first to eliminate weaknesses and later to elevate strengths. There are many routes up the mountain. Your job as coach is to find the right one.

If being a couple wasn't pressure enough, our wedding was scheduled for a few weeks after the test. With this in mind, Charmaigne had a couple of special requirements from her coach. She wanted her nose in one piece and her shins free of bruises when she walked down the aisle. The shins was a tall order because blocking low kicks for thirty minutes can play havoc with a well-turned shin. All

I could suggest was working even harder on evasive footwork and low kick drills, which she did.

With the kinks ironed out of our fighter-coach relationship, the last part of our training went well and soon it was the day of the test. Charmaigne had requested a December grading because our wedding would get in the way of summer preparations. Sensei Gavin had agreed and it was scheduled to take place in the Kilburn dojo. It seemed fitting that her test would be where I'd done mine two years earlier.

It was a crisp and clear Sunday and the traffic across central London was moving freely. Charmaigne seemed calm and focused in the seat beside me. In contrast, my palms were slipping all over the wheel. I hoped she didn't sense my anxiety. I had no idea what was causing it. Her fitness was high, her skills were all in place, and despite her lack of aggression in training, I knew she was a fighter and had no doubt she'd rise to the challenge. I could still recall the end of her shodan grading a few years earlier. I'd been tasked with holding a board for her to break. She'd been tired and ragged after four hours of gruelling action – and furious for being forced to grapple on muddy grass – and she'd chosen to break with a punch. I'd had my doubts because this was a solid one-inch block of pine and she was so light. A knife-hand or hammer-fist break would have been more reliable. A punch would have to be just right, and if she failed to break, the damage to her hand would be far greater. But what did I know? She threw her bodyweight into her punch with a savage kiai and her tight little fist went through that board like butter. I think it was the moment I fell in love with her.

Back in the car, and despite everything I knew about her, I still felt incredibly nervous. It was my first experience of the helplessness you're destined to feel as a coach. Like a parent whose child is going up on that big lonely stage, you realise there's only so much you can do and the rest is up to them. Sometimes you feel like jumping in there and doing it yourself – although not so much with the Thirty Man – but all you can do is sit on the sidelines and give encouragement.

Inside the dojo, Sensei Dan Lewis from Bristol was there to officiate alongside Sensei Gavin. Charmaigne's line would consist of fifteen fighters, all green belt or higher, and she would face each one twice. Among them were tough female fighters from Bristol and Southampton who'd come specially. DKK's first female black belt, the formidable Tracy Gallen, had also come out of semi-retirement for the event. After Tracy there were three nidans (2nd dan) and, somewhere in the line, also two male black belts to add a little extra spice.

From the beginning, Charmaigne moved smoothly. Her footwork and angles made her difficult to hit. She kept her distance, just outside striking range, and stepped in and out with a bouncing step. She was throwing plenty of punches and low-kicks with good balance and rhythm. But every so often in that tight space she was backed against the wall and took some heavy shots. I kept my coaching and my support low key, just reassuring her that she was doing everything right.

It's surprising how people see things differently. Many times fighters have felt they were performing badly while I've felt they were doing well. The reason for this is the difference between training, no matter how hard, and grading. The sense of occasion, the magnitude of the test, the presence of the chief instructors and the crowd – they all combine to create a huge drop of adrenaline. This runs through the line-up as well as the candidate, making it an experience that's impossible to replicate even in the hardest training.

These days I warn fighters beforehand: when you feel the ferocity of the line-up for the first time you must trust in your training. The fighters you're facing are far too good to let you hit and move at will. You'll get cornered and you'll get hit and it'll seem like nothing you did in training is working. At times like these, its important to have faith. Don't start casting around for 'reasons why…' Keep your head in the game and take each fight as it comes, simply doing what you trained to do. And listen to your coach, who's hopefully shouting to you that everything's alright.

After the first ten fights there was a short break and this was exactly the conversation I had with Charmaigne. She felt her game-plan wasn't working. I reassured her it was working just fine and she should just do more of the same. Looking at her, with only a hint of perspiration, I could see she still had plenty of gas left in the tank. I gave her a quick hug and then it was time for her to return to the mat.

In the next ten fights her pace showed no sign of slowing. The rate of her footwork and striking surprised even me. There was a fire in her that made me quite humble and any worries I'd had about her aggression were completely unfounded. She was throwing combinations that would put many a fresh fighter to shame.

One Bristol fighter had experience in Thai boxing and attacked hard and relentlessly. Another tall and powerful fighter threw heavy shots that thudded into Charmaigne's body. Yet another tall, rangy fighter forced her to the edge of the mat and knocked her into the crowd. Charmaigne had to be lifted and bundled back onto the mat. A fighter from Southampton came forward like a steamroller with a never-ending stream of hard punches. Charmaigne was forced to give ground but she still managed to answer with strikes of her own. After twenty fights another two-minute break was called. Again I reassured her that she was still doing just fine. She seemed a little more confident now, knowing that with only ten fights left, the finish was in sight.

But these fights were more difficult to watch. Her high work rate had begun to tell and I could see her power waning. I began to worry she'd get seriously hurt but in the last five fights, she found some new resolve and I was amazed to see fierce combinations still coming from her.

The line wasn't letting her have it her own way. One of the nidans, Karen Sheldon, caught her with a sharp front kick in the solar plexus. Charmaigne went down on one knee but moments later she was back up and fighting on. A head-kick connected moments later. 'Not the face!' I wanted to yell, but Karen had controlled the kick beautifully and it had landed neatly across the side of the jaw. Charmaigne wobbled but didn't go down. Karen touched Charmaigne's cheek in a gesture of concern that may seem deeply contradictory, and yet is so typical in DKK. These are friends pushing each other to places neither of them really want to go.

In her final fight against the incredibly tough Jay Valle, Charmaigne was battered and her energy spent. Jay backed Charmaigne up against the staircase leading to the mezzanine floor and hammered her against the iron girder that formed a hand rail. More hard shots sent Charmaigne stumbling into Sensei Gavin, standing close by, and almost under the stairs. Charmaigne took all of this with no apparent discomfort. The blows barely seemed to register. She was in the zone and nothing could harm her now. Finally Sensei Gavin heard the timekeeper's call above the din and threw himself between them to end the bout. Charmaigne faced her line-up for a formal bow. Moments later I was on my feet and holding her – not too tightly, so she could breathe – and reassuring her that she'd done the test in fine style. I was proud and humbled by what she'd done, and what we'd achieved together. Better still, she'd kept her looks for the wedding. And when we checked her shins, they'd come through with barely a blemish.

Winter Camp

The nights draw in early at this time of year. The ground is covered in a thick layer of leaves and there's a damp smoky taste in the air. The campsite is a short hop from London in Epping Forest and instead of tents, we have dorms in a scouts' hut. Later tonight we'll give up this central-heated luxury to stand out under the stars. Stories will be told around the campfire and beers shared, some trusted brands and some homebrews. Then some dodgy old unlabelled spirits will emerge and get offered around like a challenge to the unwary and the unwise. At some point a guitar might appear and anyone who can knock out a tune will take a turn. In the morning we'll go for a long walk in the forest armed with a map and compass and some cryptic directions. With heads made dull from the night before, it's easy to take a wrong turn and end up in the brambles. But eventually everyone gets back to camp and the karate training can begin.

All this is yet to come. First there's important business to take care of in the bar. Yes, there's even a bar. With drinks in hand, Sensei Gavin calls for quiet and seven people step forward to address the rest, six men and one woman. Each in turn announces his or her intention to attempt the Thirty Man Kumite next summer. A shot of single malt accompanies the declaration and much hilarity follows, fuelled by whisky and high spirits.

It's the first time this ceremony has taken place and it won't be the last. The declaration is a reflection of the subtle change that's taken place over the years. When Carl McKenzie took the first DKK Thirty Man Kumite test in 2000, he was the most experienced fighter on the field. When I took mine in 2002, Carl and Mark Salomone were the only DKK nidans in my line. Steve Jones, who'd done an epic line-up six months earlier, had returned to Canada. So while there were plenty of difficult brown and black belts to fight, the level of skill and experience was almost all lower than my own.

Not any more. At Summer Camp 2014 the last ten fighters wore the black gi that signified they had completed the Thirty Man Kumite, and there was a noticeable spike in intensity when the black gis took over. With four people passing the test in 2014, summer 2015 promised a line that included fourteen 'men in black'.

Instead of taking a place of honour near the head of the association, the nidan candidate is now seeking to enter a select club of veterans who have all gone before. These veterans are reluctant to accept new members unless they consider them worthy. And each time a new member fights his way in, the membership criteria gets tougher for those who follow.

So new protocols have been put in place to ensure candidates have time to prepare. The first of these is the request. Unlike other gradings, where candidates are told they're ready, the nidan attempt must be initiated by the candidates themselves. This puts the responsibility firmly on their shoulders. It also ensures no one ever feels forced or obliged to take the test. Those who've achieved DKK shodan are welcome to remain as a black belt as long as they please. The decision to push on through the ranks towards instructor-level and master-level is theirs alone. They've fought in the line-up more than once and know what to expect. The decision is the first dragon to face. The second is announcing the intention publicly. This happens roughly eight months before the test, which is fast becoming the minimum time needed to prepare.

Of the seven nidan candidates who raise their glasses, three are from London. One has been training with me already and I encourage the others to start soon. There's a lot to do. Strategy, tactics, technique and mind-set all take time to develop. Likewise building a new base level of fitness over the winter, so we can reach a higher peak in the summer. Quite simply, this long-sighted approach is the only way any fighter can hope to succeed against a line-up of today's calibre. The whisky does more than celebrate an important occasion. It also marks the last carefree moment before serious training must begin.

The Programme

Setting the right training programme is the second biggest factor in a good performance. Sticking to it is the first.

There's a lot to consider. The training must be geared towards the goal, namely extended full-contact kumite. Hard sparring is the closest training to the test so it's arguably the most important. However it's also the most damaging and must be handled with care. Light sparring and heavy pad-work are good alternatives because they can be done with less risk of injury and setbacks.

The place for all this and more is the dojo. So your programme must be built around regular karate classes, at least twice a week. In a good dojo there's a natural spirit of competition and camaraderie that's impossible to replicate. Like cyclists in a peloton, you get sucked along by the group and train far harder than you would on your own. Better still, you spar with the same people you'll be fighting. This gives you the chance to become familiar with the most dangerous fighters. They say familiarity breeds contempt but in sparring, familiarity breeds confidence. You learn what to expect, so nothing comes as a surprise when you're tired and hurting.

The next best form of training is with a partner. This is someone who can run through drills with you, hold pads for you, and keep you company while you get fit. Try and find someone willing to commit to regular training, perhaps someone who's considering the test in the future. Maybe there's a group that meets up at the weekend that you can join. My own coaching would come under this category of partner work.

Finally, fill the rest of your schedule with solo training designed to plug the gaps in your development. Do at least one weekly session on the heavy bag. Two is even better. A good bag session would be fifteen minutes of skipping and shadow-boxing to warm up, fifteen minutes on the bag and fifteen minutes of conditioning and stretching to finish. Total time: forty-five minutes. Leave the gym fresh enough to train again tomorrow.

Keep everything as close to fight-training as possible. Sparring and bag-work is primary, general karate is secondary, and exercises like sprints, weights and circuits come third. Don't kid yourself that other stuff like cycling and power yoga is helping. Get back to the dojo or hit the heavy bag. A detailed training programme and drills are listed in the Appendix.

I recommend five days a week as a basic structure. For example, two days of dojo training, one partner session and two days of solo training. With two rest days each week, there's less danger of overtraining. The five days needn't be the same intensity. Aim for three hard days, for example two dojo sessions and one partner session, and two lighter solo sessions. Lighter doesn't mean slow or sluggish. A good light session is intense but short. Don't be afraid to cut it down to thirty minutes from start to finish. The key is being adaptable. If you have a light session in the dojo, make up for it with a hard session of your own.

The best indication you're on the right programme is you're getting better each week. This needn't be big improvement. Slow and steady gains is the way forward in the long build up to the event. If you can do seven hard one-minute rounds in January and add one each week, you'll be doing thirty by June. I recommend this over doing thirty rounds in January, because most of these rounds will be sluggish and you'll be training at a pace that doesn't reflect the intensity of the test. You'll also take longer to recover and this will affect the rest of your training.

The five days can include morning sessions. Fifteen to thirty minutes of cardio, basics and stretching helps to limber up for the rest of the day. This should begin lightly and get more intense as your fitness grows. Perhaps three mornings a week is enough. You must be the judge of whether you're getting stronger each week.

Morning is a good time for training. Get up half an hour earlier and the time is all yours. No need to negotiate, everyone else is still asleep.

Rest days are as important as training days. With no recovery there can be no growth, and the harder you train, the harder you must rest. If you feel seriously stiff, sore and tired then do nothing and allow your batteries to recharge. Soak in a hot bath or get a sports massage. If you don't feel too tired and want to stay limber, do some gentle kata and stretch off. Avoid the temptation to push yourself to breaking point every day. Force yourself to rest so you can reach a new plateau next week.

Have one weekly 'barometer' session where you take a reading of your progress. Keep a record of your performance and try to improve each week. One extra minute on the bag. A few seconds off your run. A couple of extra push-ups, sit-ups and squats in your circuit. Small gains are best because they don't throw your training programme out of whack. If you add too much too soon, you take too long to recover. If you can't make any improvements, don't panic. Maybe you improved a lot last week and this is a consolidation week. But if your performance is worse, you need to rest and consider adjusting your schedule. Shorten your solo sessions so you're not overtraining.

This assessment and adjustment must continue throughout your training. Be attuned to your body and prepared to adapt. Over time, dojo sessions that were once punishing will start to feel quite manageable. Then you can add intensity to your other sessions or do extra rounds of pad-work and conditioning after class. The aim is always the same: small improvements each week.

Walking in the Foothills

If you were to measure your output on a graph over a week it would resemble a series of hills and valleys. Ideally the peaks get a little higher each week, like gently rising foothills leading to a mountain at the end. This process of 'walking in the foothills' goes on until you reach base camp, which is eight weeks before the test. From here there's a steep ascent that reaches a peak on the day of the test.

Each stage is important. By far the most underused and undervalued is walking in the foothills. It's where the difference between a solid performance and a great performance is made. Why? Because you have the luxury of time. Like a climber preparing for Everest, it pays to walk in the foothills. Get used to your backpack and your boots. Acclimatise to the altitude so you don't feel sick. By the time you reach Everest Base Camp you're already at 5,000m, higher than the highest Alps, and over half way to summit. The final ascent will be far steeper and tougher. But now you're free to climb without worrying about your kit – which is the last thing you need when you're clinging to a ledge 8,000m above sea level.

Kumite Training

Sparring is your single most important training method, so it's worth considering in depth to ensure you make the most of it.

First, the basics. Bring the right kit and have it handy, so you can get started right away. Don't waste time searching through your bag when you could be training.

Second, make active decisions about your sparring partners. Don't spar with beginners because they're not challenging you. Someone else can help them, you have yourself to worry about. As a nidan candidate you have certain rights and privileges that the rest should understand. These include picking your training partners. So don't be bashful about breaking up a happy couple about to spar and taking one for yourself. Better still, seek out certain fighters beforehand and ask them to find you during sparring.

Third, have an agenda with each bout. Try to get more than the simple experience of sparring. You can have two different aims in sparring: trying to win, or trying to learn. Consider which is doing the most for you. If you try to win, you'll use your most trusted techniques and try and shut down your opponent. This is good for your confidence, but it has limited value in preparing for the Thirty Man.

During the test, you'll be fighting from a position of disadvantage caused by tiredness. However thanks to all the extra training you're doing, your fitness is higher than average, so you have an advantage in the dojo. How can you replicate the tiredness of the Thirty Man Kumite? The answer is to work harder than normal in some way.

Instead of trying to close down the fast fighters, try to keep up with them. Instead of trying to evade the heavy hitters, go toe to toe with them.

Don't hit so hard that you discourage your opponent from attacking. Save your vicious strikes for the pads. You want fighters to open up on you, so don't punish them for it. Encourage them. This way you get to practise in the eye of the storm. See how long you can stay comfortable under pressure. However if you feel yourself getting hurt, hit back and dance away. This training method should build your confidence, not damage it.

Finally, remember putting yourself at a disadvantage is only for dojo sparring. During the test, go back to your winning strategy of closing down the fast guys and evading the big hitters.

Fight to your strengths and their weaknesses. Your new-found skills will serve you well in this.

Happy New Year

The Christmas break has been grey and miserable but without the snows of the last two years. It's a time for taking things a bit easy after three months of hard training. I enjoy solo training at this time of year. The windy parks and rainy fields are empty and I have them all to myself. Long runs help you keep warm when it's too cold to stop and do anything else. Just keep putting one foot in front of the other and you'll get home... eventually. Coming into the warmth, with the smell of cooking on the stove and the laughter of children in the air, I know I've done my work for the day and now I'm free to relax.

This year we've been blessed with the arrival of a new child, a baby girl whom we adopted from six months old. She's been with us for three months and we've never been happier. On Christmas Day, dressed in a little Santa suit, she gets passed around our big family faster than a box of Quality Street. We're worried it might be too much for her but she seems to take all the hugs and kisses in her stride.

We began looking into adoption a year earlier and underwent a long programme of training and assessment.

An independent social worker looked into every aspect of our lives. She interviewed friends, relations and even my ex-wife to check we were suitable. It was a tense time, so there was considerable relief when we passed. By the time I learnt a little girl had been found for us, the tension returned. Were we doing the right thing? Some of the stories we'd heard of troubled adoptions had been deeply worrying. I hoped our experience would be different.

The moment I met the little girl, I knew we'd be just fine. Judging by her happy gurgling smiles, it seemed she felt the same. The worries about adoption faded quickly and were soon forgotten. Little did I know they would resurface with a vengeance soon enough.

Meanwhile, inexorably, January comes around and with it a return to dojo discipline. Sensei Gavin serves up an extra hard warm-up to get rid of those Christmas calories. A week later something far more serious awaits the three nidan candidates: a Five Man Kumite.

Over time a typical pattern has emerged for this short, sharp, shocker of a test. The first fight is usually fast and furious but the candidate copes well. The second fight is more of the same. By the third fight, things begin to unravel. They slow down and start taking unanswered blows. They get winded. Legs get hacked and they end up on the floor. They start looking around, searching for a way out. There isn't one. They lose focus, drop their guard and this signals the beginning of the end. The fourth and fifth fights are grim affairs. Watching the candidates getting knocked down and standing up, sometimes time and again, you know exactly what they're thinking. This is five fights – how the hell am I going to fight thirty people in June?

Not every candidate suffers this badly but plenty do, and all of them are deeply affected by the experience. This is the real purpose of the test. The Five Man Kumite is a stone cold wake-up call, just in case there's any confusion about what's required between now and June.

This year, Gavin chooses five fighters to create a fair sample of brown and black belts. I stand at the edge of the mat with the rest, keen to see how the candidates perform. The first two follow the typical pattern quite closely, struggling from the third fight. I'm not surprised because as far as I know, they haven't done much extra training since winter camp. However the third candidate, Jake, has been training with me regularly and I'm hoping it'll pay off. When Jake's test begins, my hopes fade fast. He struggles from the outset and by the end of the first fight he looks to be in real trouble. I'm wondering what else to do if my coaching so far has made so little difference. But in the second fight Jake begins to assert some control. In his typically unpredictable style, he fights better and better, finishing the fifth fight tired but still standing tall and punching hard. I'm relieved for his sake, and mine.

After, he admits nerves affected him badly at the start. As time went on he managed to get them under control. This can be a problem even for the best fighters and it takes a few minutes to lose the 'freeze' effect of adrenaline and get it flowing with your movements.

I talk with all three candidates. They're at a low ebb. I tell them, somewhat lamely, not to worry. With the right training and mind-set they can get way, way better – far beyond anything they can imagine at the moment. But no matter how much I reassure them, my words sound hollow. They've encountered a new dragon, far nastier than any they've faced before. Requesting the test and announcing their intention at winter camp were hardly dragons at all. This one's hurt them and the wounds will take time to heal. Worse is the knowledge that it's still a baby compared to the monster awaiting them in June.

Total Training

Mind, body and spirit sounds like a cliché from a self-help book but it's a useful frame of reference in training. I define mind as the part of the brain that deals with calculating and understanding. Mind is logical and intelligent. Mind grasps strategy, tactics and technique. Most of the time mind controls body like a rider controls a horse. Some bodies are racehorses, some are carthorses and some are mules, but body-type isn't a major factor. Racehorses are prone to injury while mules are hardy and keep going.

A good rider is attuned to his horse. He makes it work hard but he doesn't drive it into the ground. If he notices undue tiredness or injury he stops to put things right.

Spirit is feelings that originate in the unconscious mind and manifest in the body. Consider how emotions like excitement, elation, fear, sadness, love and grief are felt in the chest and stomach. These sensations are the result of chemical secretions in the body like adrenaline and endorphins, and the nervous signals that give a tangible feeling to moods and emotions. This is why terms like 'heart' and 'guts' are associated with courage, while having the 'stomach' for something means a willingness to face up to unpleasant things.

If mind is the rider and body is the horse, spirit is the bond between the two. When it's strong, it makes the team more than the sum of its parts.

Mind, body and spirit work like the Hachiman symbol in Japanese art – three interlocking elements that flow into one. The strength of the individual elements can wax and wane. If one is weak, the other two can work together to compensate. If the mind loses its way, body and spirit can take over. This is common at the end of the Thirty Man Kumite. Likewise if the body is weak, mind and spirit can work together to push through. If the spirit is weak it usually means mind and body aren't working in harmony. Mind must usually work harder to understand body.

Like a good rider, mind needs to be strict but fair. The body is a simple creature and deserves to be treated with respect. That means training hard but also training right. Fixing the right ratio of work and recovery. Steady progress breeds success and confidence. When mind and body feel themselves working together it raises the spirits. Shihan Chris Rowen used to talk about adding thin layers of varnish and sanding each one down, rather than trying to slap on one thick layer. This way we produce a strong flexible shell that won't crack. What a good way to describe it: patiently adding layers of strength and polishing each one until it shines. This is how you start feeling good about who you are and what you do. It's also why I have little sympathy for people who over-train. It's as bad as under-training, and in some ways, more annoying. Good health is a gift. The ability to train is something precious that we don't appreciate – until we lose it. Driving your body into the ground with hours of unnecessary work is a waste and ultimately a bit cowardly. It gives you permission to say you've trained really, really hard and you can't understand why you're always struggling and constantly injured. This 'wounded warrior' approach is an indication that you want a plausible excuse to opt out. As you can probably tell, it cuts little ice with me.

The Total Fighter is mentally, physically and emotionally tough. His mind is clear on strategy and focused on attack and defence. His body is conditioned to work long and hard with good form and take punishment without undue concern. His spirit is determined to get through, come hell or high water. When mind, body and spirit are working together like this, you have a fighter to be reckoned with.

Mark Salomone – one of the first in DKK to complete the Thirty Man Kumite in 2001

Steve Jones, a memorable Thirty Man Kumite from 2002

Dominic Du Plooy (left) final fight against me, Summer 2006

Tunde Oladimeji preparing to face Neil 'Goliath' Grove after twenty fights, Summer 2007

Facing the long line: Steve Power, Dragosh Voiculescu and
Simon Mackown, 2011

Simon Mackown enjoys fighting Rob Curtis, Summer 2011

Mind: Strategy

When a pro fighter prepares for a fight, he doesn't train the same way every time. He studies his opponent's style and works with his trainer to create a winning strategy. They look at the opponent's strengths and work out how to counter them. They examine the opponent's weaknesses and work out how to exploit them. In short, they train style against style.

With thirty different fighters you can't be too specific about individual styles, however there are some things you know to be true. Most of the time, you'll be more tired than your opponent. So if you plan to use brute force to get through, your strategy is unlikely to succeed. Instead you should draw inspiration from smaller, lighter fighters who rely on mobility and technical excellence.

The heavier you are, the less vital mobility is, but good footwork is always important. Some fighters, usually with a heavyset frame, have only one direction and that is forwards. This isn't ideal for a test where evasion is a key skill, however it's better than standing still. Pressing forward gives you natural momentum and creates a moving target that's harder to hit. If you fight this way, so be it. Just make sure you can throw a lot of punches because you'll be in striking range most of the time.

It's important to have a clear and attainable objective for the test. Some might say it should be to win each fight. This is positive, which is good, but trying to beat every opponent can quickly unravel even the best fighter.

Conversely, not getting beaten or 'actively defending yourself' is too negative and engenders the wrong mind-set. The objective I like is to control the fight. That doesn't mean you have to be as busy as your opponent, you just have to be better. The inferior fighter throws a lot of leather and only some of it sticks. The superior fighter throws less but makes every shot count.

Training with the Jeet Kune Do master Bob Breen, I heard a concept that resonated deeply with me. *One is always the hunter.* Watch two people fighting and you can usually see who is the hunter. He isn't necessarily the most aggressive or the most active. A big game hunter doesn't fight a tiger or wrestle a bear. He uses the right tools for the job, usually a big accurate gun. Whether he's stalking or shooting or setting traps, he is the predator and the tiger and the bear have become the prey. He forces them to move, lures them with bait, drives them with noise. He calls the shots. He is the hunter.

You control the fight not by throwing punches and kicks, but by seeing the bigger picture and, like the hunter, weighing everything in your favour. By controlling distance, timing, and position, you get to throw your strikes without being stuck.

However when your body is exhausted and your mind and spirit are hanging by a thread, you need to cling to a simple formula. Controlling the fight is a little vague and hard to define. Controlling distance, timing and position is more concrete, but it's still a lot to remember when you're in the fray. Let's boil it down to its core: a simple, memorable strategy that you can remember even in the most dire of circumstance.

Hit. And avoid being hit.

Still too complicated? Perhaps. Let's make it simpler, more memorable – a mantra you'll never forget.

How do we avoid being hit? *Hit and run?*

It's clear and catchy but I don't like the idea of running. There's no running away in the Thirty Man. There is evasion but that's different. Evasion keeps you in the fight and enables you to strike back. So how about something more positive?

How about: *Hit and move.*

Simple, clear, positive. A mantra to guide you in all your training? I think so. Memorable, even in the most dire circumstances? I hope so.

Mind: Tactics

While a strategy is an overall plan to achieve an objective, tactics are the steps you take on the way. To control the fight you must hit your opponent with meaningful strikes. This is Yang. But your opponent won't simply allow you to open up on him. So you need tactics that enable you to land clean, hard strikes. These are Yin.

There are several ways to strike hard. The simplest is to step in and strike. Some fighters don't have a decent guard, which is like going out and leaving the front door wide open. Unsurprisingly, these fighters are rare in DKK and you can't expect to face them in the Thirty Man Kumite.

The next way is to create an opening by using slip-timing: misleading your opponent into thinking you're backing off and then coming forward. Most fighters have a noticeable rhythm of footwork moving forwards and backwards. By indicating you're going one way and going the other you can sometimes land a strike when the opponent isn't expecting it.

Even better is to create some sort of small advantage before you strike. Get a better angle from the side or 45 degrees. This is done by moving yourself onto a new line or forcing your opponent off-line. Often a bit of both. The easiest way is to wait until he attacks. Kicks are ideal because they commit his balance more than punches. Pick up a front kick and redirect it off-line. When your opponent lands, he's facing away from you. Pounce on a chance like this and commit your strikes, then move away before he can respond.

In all strike-training, you must be disciplined from the outset. Bag-work and pad-work are one-dimensional – 'Yang'. You can bang away to your heart's content and it feels good, standing tough and hitting hard. But it's a dangerous habit to get into. In reality your opponent's counter-strikes will be affecting you severely. Not only will they hurt, and eventually numb, but they'll disrupt your body mechanics and make it difficult to hit hard.

For this reason, all your strike-training must take account

of Yin which, rather than blocking, is best understood as 'not being struck'. That means keeping distance from the bag and actively stepping in and out of range every time. This trains you to control when contact takes place. Strike on the way in so you always 'enter with a bang'. If you enter without striking you're more likely to walk onto counters. Landing the first punch causes disruption at the beginning of the contact and makes it harder for your opponent to strike. Always 'exit off your last punch' to avoid counters. Get the knack of using your last strike to push yourself away.

Your punches can be singles or combinations but the key is to control distance. This builds good habits that grow into a natural fighting savvy.

As well as pad drills, work on reaction drills against the most common attacks – front kicks, round kicks, low kicks, straight punches and knees. For front and mid-level kicks use footwork and evasion with a counter. For low kicks – the most damaging of all – use blocking, disrupting and evading drills – all with counters. Work these slowly as flow drills and build up speed each week so your reactions become fast, fluid and natural. Some example drills are given in the Appendix.

Also work on 'tapping hands' – standing close and lightly tapping the top of each punch as it comes in. This drill builds reaction speed and awareness. It's surprising how easy it is to read your attacker once you get in tune with his movements. This ability to 'read' attacks is one of the most crucial skills to hone in preparation for the Thirty

Man. Once these drills are in place, add drills to prevent grabs, avoid knee-strikes and break free from the clinch – also listed in the Appendix.

It's worth noting that only one of these drills involves what would normally be considered 'blocking' and even then, it's based on 'receiving' a low-kick – like catching a cricket or baseball and throwing it back – rather than crunching against it. Clashing shins against thirty fighters is not a sound tactic.

Give attacks only the minimum attention before focusing on your return strike. Develop small parries and subtle foot movement that's just enough to negate the attack and put you in a position to punish. Yin and Yang together, Yang: striking, Yin: not being struck.

Mind: Technique

While fitness is vital, you can't pass this test with fitness alone. There's a limit to how fit you can get and besides, you're fighting thirty fit people. You can't hope to out-punch or out-manoeuvre them all.

Unlike fitness, which is more or less finite, technique is infinite. You can hone and perfect technique over time and the scope for improvement is almost limitless. Fitness delivers performance through power and endurance. Technique delivers it from the other side: efficiency – yet another example of Yin, or 'enabling' something more.

Imagine you're in a motor racing team that competes in a

2000cc race. You produce the most powerful engine you can make. But there's a size limit, so after this the only way to make the car faster is to make it more efficient. Strip it down. Ensure every moving part is clean and oiled. Make sure the axles are straight and the wheels are spinning evenly. Check the oil's flowing smoothly. Remove all unnecessary baggage. These small gains in efficiency are hard to find but they're the way forward once your engine is at maximum.

It's worth considering what makes good technique. As a rule of thumb, good technique uses physics to its most effective. The basic drills of kihon and kata allude to the optimum body mechanics of a technique, if you know where to look. The placement of the feet, the posture and alignment of the body, the shift of bodyweight through the technique – these are coded in kihon and kata. The refinement of technique is a never-ending drive towards perfection that can't be reached, but you can get a little closer each time.

We're not talking about every movement in every kata – that's a lifetime's work in itself – but rather a handful of key movements used in sparring: footwork, punching, kicks, parries and basic clinch-work. This selection is small enough that, given time, you can make serious improvements in efficiency.

The mark of good technique is it shouldn't require great effort. Like a workman selecting the right tools for the job, let the technique do the work. The workman doesn't use his whole arm to wield a hammer. He holds it at the base and allows the length and weight of the hammer to do the work. Try and do the same with your toolkit of punches, blocks and kicks.

Take some time to assess each one. Feel where you get maximum effect for minimum effort. The key is usually to engage as much bodyweight as possible. Shifting bodyweight engages the big muscles of the legs and torso and requires less work from the smaller muscles of the arms. Better still, moving the whole body fits with our strategy of hit and move. Similarly, with circular techniques like hooks and round kicks, a bigger rotation of hips and shoulders means less muscular effort is required to achieve the same result.

Make sure your breathing is big, loud and fluid. If it's too quiet, you're not filling up with energy. If you're holding or catching your breath, you're tense in the body and this hinders momentum.

Strip away effort and see what results you can get from loud, relaxed breathing and a simple shifting of weight. It's surprising how hard you can hit without trying, if you get it right. Out of every ten punches, one or two usually land harder than the rest. Your partner or coach should point these out so you can identify what you did and learn to repeat it.

Look for power with less effort. Usually it boils down to three things: throwing bodyweight from a bit further back, hitting exactly on target, and locking on impact.

Throwing bodyweight from further back means there's a feeling of falling into the technique, like stumbling into someone and knocking them over while you stay upright. Hitting on target is vital. If your strike lands slightly left or right, your momentum slips off and lacks penetration. That means if you hit the pad ten times, all ten punches should be in exactly the same place.

When it comes to impact, notice I don't say tensing on impact but rather locking. While tensing is fine and indeed good, at this stage we're looking for maximum efficiency through the use of bodyweight. A simple locking of the arm and body is all that's required to drop bodyweight into a strike. We practise this way for a while until natural momentum can be felt and harnessed. Later, we add venom to our strikes and ram them home with tension. But for now we're working on technique and the mark of good technique is, as the old aftershave ads used to say: you don't have to try too hard.

Mind: Visualisation

Visualisation is one of the most powerful training tools. Where the mind leads, the body follows. But where should the mind lead? The right vision sets a path for the body to go along.

Visualisation begins early in karate. In kihon basics, we aim at an imaginary opponent the same size as ourselves. In kihon-ido (moving basics) we need to visualise important lines or meridians to help us understand our bodies and the pathways to our target. The Vertical

Centre Line runs down through our head and torso. The Horizontal Centre Line runs from our belly button to the opponent's. The Tramlines run like train tracks, shoulder width apart, from our feet. When we punch, we visualise the path of the middle knuckle. If it's a straight punch we aim to deliver it along a straight line. If it's a round punch, we aim to produce a smooth curve.

Seeing these lines clearly is fundamental to both accuracy and power. A technique delivered in a wobbly line is less powerful. Moreover in the heat of battle, targets appear and disappear with bewildering speed. You need to see an opening developing and your path to hitting it instantly. That way your body can react without thinking.

As a coach, it pays to check if your fighter can see these lines and follow them clearly. You can usually tell by watching them perform kihon ido. Make sure they are tidy and straight, hitting the same points each time, with eyes and strikes focused on one spot. Another way to tell is hitting the pads. A fighter who can see and follow the meridians will hit the pad consistently on target and his body won't drift left or right (unless you move). If you notice a lot of shifting and drifting, spend time on kihon-ido during the warm-up to develop kime (focus). Make sure his feet, hips, hands and gaze are all exactly where they should be. Take time, under stress-free conditions, to hit these targets correctly. It'll pay dividends when you return to pad-work and sparring.

In kihon we use visualisation to help us understand technique and move the body correctly. However visualisation can also be used to build spirit and dial up training to the max. I deal with this aspect of visualisation in the section on spirit.

Body: Fitness

There are different kinds of fitness. A powerlifter might be able to press fifty kilos over his head many more times than a tennis player, but he would quickly flag on the tennis court. The tennis player's physique is shaped by the training he does and the actions he repeats. The hand and the arm that hold the racquet are especially strong from countless hours of work. The legs are used for lunging and changing direction quickly, short sprints and fast footwork. A boxer has similarly good footwork and his shoulders and back are shaped by the punching he does. While all three athletes have fitness, each is specific to his own sport.

The fitness we want is fighting fitness, so take lessons from how a pro fighter trains. A boxer goes for a run in the morning, followed by limbering up exercises. In the evening he does skipping, shadowboxing, bag-work, sparring, circuits and stretching. This is repeated, with a few variations, five days a week. His trainer might work on focus mitts one day, heavy bag another, lighter sparring or harder sparring, but they're variations on the same themes. Boxers have been competing professionally for over a hundred years and in that time they've learnt what works and what doesn't. Twelve three-minute rounds is not far off thirty one-minute rounds. Boxers have great cardio, they can hit and move all day. They're strong but they don't carry more muscle than they need because it's tiring. Ignore their methods at your peril.

Don't put your name down for the London Marathon. Don't start a powerlifting programme you found on the internet. Don't do yoga to improve your kicks. Train like a fighter. Just keep in mind the specifics of the Thirty Man Kumite: all punches are to the body, so train on the heavy bag rather than focus mitts, and work kicks too.

The question of weights is a good one. I recommend building weights into a circuit after your bag-work. Instead of working towards pure strength, which means heavy weights, low reps and plenty of rest, work towards power-endurance. Start with a light-to-mid barbell and pump out as many squats, shoulder presses, bent-over rows and deadlifts as you can with no rest. Engage your whole body to keep the bar moving. Take a few seconds' rest and do a set of push-ups and sit-ups. Then repeat with a mid-to-heavy bar and another set of push-ups and abs.

This continuous work resembles the physicality of a fight more closely than a pure strength workout. The constant pushing and shoving with no rest is a killer and it won't take long to feel exhausted. Do this circuit twice a week and add weight, reps and sets as you get stronger. By all means add other exercises too, including chin-ups, dips, battle-ropes and the like, but keep everything moving fast and hard with short recovery times. CrossFit is good for this sort of training but don't neglect your bag-work and sparring because of it.

Cardio is important too. Road-running, sprints and hill-sprints are all good, but don't do so much that you feel drained when you get to the dojo. All fitness work should enhance your sparring and pad-work, not detract from it. The goal is small gains in each area, built up over time. That way they stay with you and stand up to testing when the going gets tough – which it will, soon enough.

Body: Footwork

Imagine you've bought a piece of land and you're planning to build a house. The first job for the builders is to level the ground and lay the foundations. The foreman says they're ready to begin construction but when you check, the foundations don't look level. The foreman says the ground was tricky and this is as good as it gets. He's keen to start building because there's a lot to do. What do you do?

Personally, I would fire the foreman, and if need be his whole crew, rather than build on sloping ground. No matter how well-constructed, the whole house will be under stress because it's not resting on solid foundations.

Footwork and ring-craft are the foundations of a total fighter. Better still, footwork exercises make the perfect warm-up. Do at least five minutes every session and up to fifteen minutes to build cardio and natural movement.

Make sure you're always moving in a fighting stance until it happens without conscious thought. This is vital because you need to focus your attention on your opponent, not your feet.

Natural movement is something I come back to again and again. Like walking, most of us can walk without thinking about it, but we weren't born this way. Anyone who's seen a baby getting on its feet knows that walking is a skill. It takes muscular development, balance and technique. If you're in an accident that keeps you off your feet for a long time your body needs to re-learn how to walk by strengthening the muscles and re-forming the neural pathways that move the legs.

For a fighter, moving in fighting stance is the new walking. Fighting stance – with one leg forward and one leg back, balance even and a guard in place – is the optimum position from which to fight. Any other position is what the Americans call 'sub-optimal'. If you see an opponent in a sub-optimal position, attack. If you put yourself in a sub-optimal position, beware.

Holding a static fighting stance is easy. The difficult bit is adjusting it constantly with regard to your opponent. This constant changing of the distance and angle between you is often the deciding factor in a fight. It's how the superior fighter dominates a less experienced opponent. Controlling distance, timing and angles puts you in a better position to attack and your opponent in a difficult position to defend. Learning to use distance, timing and angles is time-consuming but well worth the investment.

This is where very traditional karate can be a bit limiting. While the fighting stances and transitions are well drilled in kihon and kata, the little shuffles, hops and skips in between must be developed in free-flow training. Begin by marking out a ring and moving around in fighting stance. Keep the stance taut but not stiff. Think of moving on sports suspension rather than bouncing around like an old French car. It's fine to switch from left to right but stay in fighting stance. Use the Palm to Palm Drill, listed in the Appendix, to practise.

The other element of footwork is ring-craft. This means using the fighting area to your advantage. If you're in the centre of the ring, you can move freely. If you back your opponent against the edge, he can't move any further back. And if you can put him in a corner, you have even more advantage because he can't move back, left or right. This restricts his movement and makes him easier to hit. For the same reason, you must be wary of being backed against the ropes or cornered. If you feel yourself backed up, it's too late. You need to slip to the side and circle away before being trapped.

This is trickier than it sounds because when you're fighting, you can't afford to look around. You must keep your focus on your opponent. That means relying on peripheral vision to tell you when it's time to slip and circle. Building this awareness takes practice but it pays big dividends. Use exercises like the Dalek Drill (outlined in the Appendix) to learn to control the area. Make sure to keep this in mind when you're shadow-boxing. Visualise your opponent coming towards you like a dalek and keep your focus on him at all times. Don't flit from side to side as if you're fighting multiple opponents. Don't spin around doing pirouettes – this isn't ballet. Hold your focus on your opponent. Always. When things get nasty and you're hurting it's incredibly tempting to look away. If you do, it's the beginning of the end. You'll get hit harder and, worse still, you won't see it coming. Instead, train your brain to hold focus at every opportunity by setting ironclad mental discipline from the start.

Body: Striking

The second section of the pyramid is working inside striking range. We begin with reaction drills to key attacks like front and round kick. These two movements require two vital aspects of footwork, slipping and blending. Slipping is moving to the side and slightly forward. Blending is moving in a circle with the attack. Slipping and blending are useful against any number of attacks because attacks either come in a straight line or a curve. Slipping and blending are better than blocking because by evading with your body, your hand remains free to strike.

Next we work on what I call Low Kick Management. I give it a name because it's so important. Low kicks are devastating and a fighter with dead legs becomes a sitting duck for punishment. The strategy of 'hit and move' will help to avoid some low kicks but not all. Your opponent will catch up with you. When he does and the kicks start flying, there are still things you can do.

The first principle of Low Kick Management is to use your legs to defend your legs. Keep your hands up to defend against hands (blocking low kicks with your arm is asking to have it broken). Your legs must learn patterns of movement designed to prevent, disrupt and evade low kicks. Think of these as dance steps with a hyper aggressive partner. There are only a few steps to learn but you must know them well because this dance can go on all night.

The first step, and worst, is blocking with the shin. Work on soft-blocking to avoid clashing shins with thirty fighters. Rather than a crunching block, think of 'catching and throwing back', as you would with a cricket- or baseball. Start with the shin forward and bring it back to arrest momentum. Turn the foot inwards slightly to avoid bone on bone. The 'throwing back' motion sends your bodyweight forward so add a two-punch combination after each block to create a fast-flowing drill.

The second step is disrupting. As the low kick comes, kick inside the opponent's supporting leg. His kick may start earlier, but you're kicking off the front foot and your target is closer. The kicks often land at the same time. That's fine because instead of eating a hard kick, you disrupt his power and land one of your own.

The third step is evading – stepping back and allowing the kick to pass in front of you – then kicking the leg that's just landed. This is not a backward step as such, but rather a bounce-back and kick.

Some fighters pick up these drills quickly. Others take time to get them working. Make sure you can do your drills correctly in a flowing sequence before moving on.

These footwork and reaction drills should form the first 15 to 20 minutes of your training and serve as a warm up. Do them light and sharp, with good crisp form. Then move onto the second phase of training which is more explosive: striking. Use a heavy bag or kick-shield rather than Thai pads because it's more like striking the body. Whether you're alone or with a partner, all striking drills must be performed in context. That means remembering that if you can reach your opponent, he can reach you. With this in mind, set yourself certain rules that must be obeyed at all times.

First, you must stay outside striking range unless you're hitting. Never stand near the bag without unloading. Never wander into striking range without striking. Always 'enter with a bang' and that way you control the timing of each exchange. You're initiating and you're controlling. Your first strike should be hard enough to disrupt and hamper his ability to retaliate. Whether you're throwing one punch or five, always exit on your last strike. Use it to push yourself away to avoid getting hit on the way out. Sticking to these rules helps you to develop a rhythm and style that makes you savvy and hard to hit.

Kumite, at this level, isn't a fair exchange where you give your opponent a sporting chance. You hit them. They don't hit you. Everything has to be on your terms. You are the hunter.

Work long and hard to develop a good lead hand. A hard first punch makes everything easier. More important, it shows an appreciation of distance and timing that makes all the difference over thirty rounds. Use straight punches rather than hooks because you stay further from your opponent and you can get away quicker.

On the kick-shield, work one-minute rounds of lead-hand punches, stepping in and out each time. Once these are landing hard, move onto reverse-hand punches and combinations of two, three, four and five. Use in-and-out footwork between each combination. Then work front kicks, round kicks and low kicks. Later add hooks and uppercuts, which are useful when you're in close. When kicking, watch that the guard stays in place. It should swing in a counter-motion to the kick, but don't let the hands go outside shoulder-width or drop to your waist because this leaves you exposed.

These rounds are not about intensity, yet. They are about correct form. Good form is good technique. Good technique is good body mechanics. Good body mechanics generates more power with less effort, keeping momentum flowing naturally rather than having to kick-start it from scratch each time. All this allows you to strike harder for longer while using less energy. When you're fighting thirty people, you need every drop of effort to count.

It's okay to stop and improve technique. Or have a breather so you can maintain good form for longer. The beauty of walking in the foothills is you have time to develop your form. As it improves each week, go a little longer, a little harder, and let your fitness grow naturally. Aim to have good form and base-level fitness in place eight weeks before the test. Take a couple of extra rest days because after this, things need to get serious and form had better hang on for dear life.

Body: Conditioning

Once your footwork and pad-work is done, finish your session with conditioning circuits and body toughening. Include the Big Four: legs (squats, lunges), chest (push-ups), abs (sit ups) and back (dorsal raises). Keep up a busy pace changing between the four. Add intensity with sprints between sets and plyometrics like jump squats and take-off push-ups. If you have weights, include them too. Squats, shoulder press, bent-over rows and deadlifts are all good. Do each exercise hard until you lose form and then move straight onto the next. Work in one minute rounds with fifteen seconds rest in between and do a bit more each week.

Body-toughening should be mixed in with the circuits but do a circuit first to pump the muscles before they get struck. I use a version of Sanchin-testing adapted for kumite, detailed in the Appendix. This kind of training must be managed carefully. There's an argument to say it's unnecessary because we should train to evade blows, not take them. As you can probably tell, I have some sympathy with this view. However you won't be able to avoid taking heavy blows and on balance, it's better to be prepared.

This kind of conditioning works on two levels. At its most basic, muscle and bone do get conditioned to impact over time, just like walking barefoot eventually toughens the soles of the feet. However the idea of battering the body until it loses all sensation can't be good or healthy. If you hit too hard too soon, you'll bruise up and these injuries will cause more pain rather than less. Worse, they'll affect your ability to train the next day. So it's important to start light and build up.

What we're really training is the more advanced level: gearing the body's reaction to strikes. There's a knack to taking heavy blows that involves coordinating three things at once. The first is breathing out on impact, which contracts the muscles and expels air to stop you getting winded. The second is tensing the muscles in the area of impact to shield your internal structure. The third is to allow a little bit of give to ride the blow. This is tricky because the second skill is tensing and the third skill is relaxing. However if you know the meaning of 'Go-ju' you'll know the combination of hard and soft is fundamental to our style of karate. The only real way to develop this ability is, as always, to train it. If you're the coach or partner who's striking the fighter, remember he's just done rounds of pad-work and circuits, so give him a chance to develop this skill. Start light and train towards success, not failure. Your fighter needs to learn to take in breath and relax between combinations, so give him a chance. Vary your combinations but don't be too tricksy. Telegraph the shots, especially at first, so he can see what's coming and prepare. It's surprising how much more he'll be taking in a few weeks' time. Then you can open up.

In many ways this is a reaction drill like any other. However the fighter hasn't had time to evade, block or disrupt so there's only one reaction left: brace for impact. It's not ideal but it will happen, more times than either of you would like.

This drill is also great for developing the mental strength to stay focused under pressure. Tired and hurting, forced to stand still and simply take blows, the fighter is learning to keep watching what's happening – even when he doesn't like it, not one bit. It's all part of learning to read your opponent and get advanced warning of attacks. Whether you deal with those attacks by evading with silky smooth footwork or you're forced to simply brace for impact depends on how well you trained and how tired you are. As long as there are no surprises, that's all that really matters.

Spirit: Emotion

Spirit – in martial arts terms at least – needn't be mystical or religious. Just think of it as your emotional state. It's less about what you're thinking and more about how you're feeling.

Spirit is by far the trickiest thing to coach. You can train the mind by learning strategy, tactics and technique. You can train the body by performing the right exercises. It's much harder to change feelings and emotions. They're soft and intangible. They don't respond to reason because they're not rational or logical. Moods can be low despite everything going well. Spirits can be high even in the most dire circumstances.

Emotions don't originate from the rational part of the brain. They come from the murky lower part: the subconscious. As the word implies, we're not aware of this aspect of our own mind. One of the deepest lessons of the test is understanding this and developing a new working relationship with this hidden aspect of ourselves.

In the murky territory of emotions, each of us is different. Our emotional make-up is largely a product of our parents and our upbringing. Some of us were told we were brilliant even when we weren't. Some of us struggled to get praise no matter how hard we tried. As grown-ups, we like to think our actions are guided by logic and reason. The more enlightened among us know that's far from true.

There's an old joke about a boss interviewing three women for a job as his secretary. On his desk there's a folder marked 'Urgent' and at some point in each interview he leaves the room. When he returns, he asks the women if they looked inside. The first says she didn't because it might have been confidential. The second says she did, but she saw a hand-written letter marked 'confidential' and put it back. The third says she's typed up the letter and printed it out ready for him to sign. Which of the three does he employ? The answer, of course, is one with the biggest tits.

Not funny, but sadly there's a ring of truth in there. Our gut – or some other part of the body – makes the real decisions for us. We want something nice so we invent a reason why we need it. We don't want something nasty so we justify why it's not for us. That's not to say the gut is always wrong. We should listen to our instincts because they're often right. But we must also be aware how susceptible we are to fears and cravings that can easily drive us off the path we choose.

Recently the idea of Emotional Intelligence has been become popular. Some experts consider it more important than IQ. In a nutshell, it's the ability to recognise feelings in ourselves and others and act accordingly. You can see how this ability would be useful in both life and work, and it's certainly useful in karate. Faced with a fearsome test like the Thirty Man Kumite, any fighter will experience unusual levels of emotional turmoil. Learning to cope is an important aspect of training.

This begins by expecting these feelings and knowing they'll come. Soon they'll begin chipping away at our rational minds and urging us to make excuses. The next step is to call in the Mind Police, who are on the lookout for these 'Subversive Elements'. Then an interrogation can commence:

So, Mr Powell... (spoken in the voice of Agent Smith from the Matrix) ...you have put in an application to miss training tonight?

I was thinking about it, yes.

You say you have an injury...

Yes, my finger is swollen and I don't want to make it worse.

I've been looking through your file. You missed class two weeks ago. Reason given: 'working late'.

It was a pitch, I had no choice.

We always have a choice, Mr Powell...

It may seem a harsh way to treat yourself but these are extraordinary circumstances. A severe test awaits and the harder you train, the less damage you'll take. So do yourself a favour and talk to the Mind Police.

They, in turn, must be firm but fair. If the reason is valid they must acknowledge it so negotiations can begin. If it's an injury, can it be strapped up? Can you train around it? Can you avoid sparring but do the rest? If you're exhausted, then be honest about why. Have you just done three hard days in a row? Then take a well-earned break. Have you been out partying? Then the Mind Police should show no mercy. Why do you have to work late?

Can you come in early tomorrow instead? Did you mess around all day when you could have got things finished? These days most of us have some flexibility in our working hours. Block out Monday and Wednesday evenings in your calendar and don't accept late afternoon meetings. Work harder on other days to make up for this. Consider telling your boss and your team what's happening. You'd be surprised how people get behind you once they understand what you're doing. Are you really going to blame your wife or girlfriend? Your husband or boyfriend? Have you worked harder recently to keep them sweet? Why not? You should. You must.

This process of self-examination, assessment and negotiation is on-going. If you're feeling very tired and thinking of missing one of your solo sessions, try warming up and see how you feel. If your energy levels lift then get a session in. But if you still feel drained, don't think twice. Pack up and go home. Rest and recharge, so you can train again soon.

If you have a cold or flu, take time off. It can be worrying to miss training but pushing yourself with a virus is dangerous and just delays recovery. Take a break of anything from two days to a week or more depending on severity. Look on the bright side: the sooner you recover, the sooner you can get back to training. The rest will allow injuries to heal and your whole body to come back fresh and strong. Viruses are a common annoyance during preparation but rare during the actual test when your adrenaline levels are high. They tend to strike when your body's at a low ebb.

There's another side to pre-test emotions that's all too easy to forget. That is the positive emotion that you should be feeling too. It pays to remind yourself (or your fighter) of the reasons for taking the test. To train like a pro fighter and reach a physical peak you're unlikely to reach again. To show what you're made of and discover new depths in yourself. To do something truly awe-inspiring – a once-in-a-lifetime achievement. To join an elite brotherhood. To pass an important milestone on your journey in karate. These ideas should excite and inspire you. Or if you want something simpler, just think how good that first beer's going to taste when it's done.

Spirit: Belief

It helps to know that negative thoughts assail everyone, not just you. They're perfectly natural. Better still, there are methods you can use to keep nerves under control. This way you can cultivate a level of self-respect and confidence you couldn't imagine before, building that vital quality of self-belief.

The first and most fundamental exercise is never to show tiredness. Make it an ironclad rule. You will never put your hands on your knees, sigh loudly, lean against a wall or look up at the sky. You'll give no indication that you're tired or hurting. You will not look like you're trying hard and you will seek no one's approval for your effort. Instead of looking inward and expressing the pain you think you feel, look outwards at an opponent, real or imaginary, and stay frosty. If you're being drilled hard by a coach, partner or sensei, make him believe that no matter how hard he works you, he'll never break you. This mind-set is vital to eradicate the cancer of self-pity. Allow self-pity to seep into your training and it will sink you in your test.

More advanced exercises in building belief should come later in your programme. That's because belief must be built on solid foundations. If you haven't stepped up your training yet, you shouldn't be feeling ready. You know whether you're in the best shape of your life or whether you've been cutting corners. That's why as a coach, I delay building confidence until I feel the fighter is shaping up and his fitness is taking off. That's the time to start adding the hard outer shell of self-belief. We do this with that most useful of all training tools: visualisation.

After the warm up and before pad-work, walk along an imaginary line of thirty fighters. Call out the names of the people you see. At first, you might struggle with this. There seems to be a mental barrier to speaking names aloud, perhaps because it makes things personal and real. It's a barrier worth breaking. Repeat this exercise every week until you get a clear image of your line: the names, the faces, the belts, the order. This vivid imagery will make you nervous... and that's exactly what you want. The flutter of nerves you feel is adrenaline dropping. Adrenaline can be your best friend or your worst enemy depending on when it comes. The good news is this is the perfect time for it. Adrenaline is a natural performance-enhancing drug that enables you to move faster and hit harder, so unleash it now and take your training to new heights.

There's another benefit, too. The more adrenaline you drop in training, the less you drip-feed when you're resting. Adrenaline that doesn't get used up stays in your system and causes the symptoms of anxiety: butterflies in the stomach, cold sweats, nausea. There's only so much anxiety you can feel in a day and the more you explore in training, the easier it is to relax afterwards.

Before hitting the pads, imagine certain fighters before you. It's surprising how you'll change your style and raise your intensity. Choosing the best fighters tends to bring out the best in you. Once you're striking with good form and sustained aggression, it's time to take your pad-work to the next level. Now, don't picture someone you know but rather a generic body of muscle and bone. Imagine your blows breaking ribs and shattering bones. Try and create ferocity and animal arousal. Strike with venom and bad intention. Develop what the boxer Carl Froch calls 'spite'.

If this sounds like a worrying training method for a martial artist, rest assured that it's just that – a training method. In sparring, and in the test, bow to your opponent and show him proper respect. Always. You should be hitting hard but injury shouldn't be your intention. This is a training method for pad-work because pads feel no pain.

You can't hurt them but neither can they hurt you – so you can be lulled into training in a stupor. This method of visualisation sets a fire in your belly and keeps you striking harder for longer. Better still, it changes how you feel about striking. Rather than being a difficult and tiring exercise you're forced to do, it becomes a skill or craft you enjoy. There's no better incentive to train than loving your work.

Spirit: Dragons

The fears that lie coiled and dormant in all of us are sure to rise as the test approaches. So be prepared. Expect little order or reason to these fears. They come from the murky subconscious mind where dreams, and nightmares, originate.

After my Thirty Man Kumite I realised the truth to the saying that our biggest fear is the unknown. When we haven't actually experienced something, it's left to our imagination to decide how bad it's going to be. The imagination is a powerful tool and it can easily get carried away, creating levels of hell that simply aren't real. The way to avoid this is, wherever possible, to become familiar with the thing you fear. In the home that is your mind, don't walk about in circles wondering what's lurking in the dark and musty cellar. Grab a flashlight and go explore.

Better still, bring someone you trust to watch your back.

That means talking to fighters who have been there before. Being open with your coach, your training partner and your sensei. It doesn't mean sharing your fears with every idiot who asks how you're doing. As far as they're concerned, you're doing just fine. Don't confide in your spouse or partner either, unless they've done the test too. You'll just freak them out. But find someone you can confide in, even if that person is yourself.

Speaking a fear aloud is a big step towards facing it. Get it out in the open, examine it and becoming familiar with it. Take it away from the imagination and into the real world. Now your rational mind can begin to create coping mechanisms. Don't imagine these fears will ever vanish because they won't. Your aim is simply to get them under control.

As the test draws near, I encourage candidates to consider, one by one, all the things that will happen and all the things that might happen. Better still, write them down in a series of FAQs (Fearfully Asked Questions) that goes something like this:

Q: How will I feel the night before my line-up?
Q: What if I hurt my hand the day before the test?
Q: How will I feel when I see thirty fighters waiting for me?
Q: What if a dangerous fighter I wasn't expecting joins the line-up?

The list should be long and detailed. Don't leave anything

to the imagination. Consider every bad, stupid, worrying and annoying thing that can and will plague you in the run-up to the test. Unhelpful remarks from friends and family. Thoughtless questions from other fighters. That so-called mate who shows you a video of someone breaking his leg in a fight. That last-minute advice that conflicts with your strategy. Worrying comments from your seniors or even your own beloved sensei.

Visualise the beginning of the test. The moment sensei tells you to go and get ready. The walk up to your tent. The tying of the gi and belt. Stepping onto the Field of Truth. The line of fighters – so long it can barely fit on one side of the field. Explore each fear fully and often until it becomes familiar.

The answers you develop should be your own. The only proviso is each one must be clear and positive. Underlying all of these fears and concerns is the knowledge that you are ready to do this thing. Your sensei, whom you trust, believes you are ready. You've seen other people get through. You'vc trained long and hard. The final hurdle is getting your mind to accept that this test, and the nidan grade, is yours for the taking.

I get the candidates to formulate their own questions and answers. I'm not looking for any particular answer, only that they have a positive outcome in each scenario. If they miss out an obvious question, I encourage them to consider it and formulate an answer. What I'm really looking for are niggling doubts that need to be resolved. We're working to create the worst case scenario so there are no nasty surprises.

A strange fighter appears from a different club.

Welcome to my line-up.

An old nemesis turns up out of the blue.

You want to fight me? Get in line.

A heavyweight champion appears.

One more won't hurt. Much.

In your mind you're training to fight the hardest line-up you can imagine. And you're still going to get through. The kudos of facing such a fierce line-up will be all the greater once you've done it. Being prepared for the worst means there are no nasty surprises on the day, and anything less seems like a bonus.

Often your general fear will manifest as a particular fear that can seem quite obscure. Charmaigne was worried about getting bruised shins. This was a very real concern for her that she mentioned all the time. Others have worried about one particular fighter, often not the most dangerous, or getting hit in one particular spot.

At the risk of sounding like an amateur Freud, these fears often relate to traumatic episodes in the past, moments when the fighter felt helpless in some way. We each have our own fears and phobias. We each see different dragons, coloured by our own imagination.

As a coach, I try to address each fighter's fear, no matter how strange or unusual, and develop coping strategies. I return to this fear each week so it becomes familiar. I try and bring the fighter closer to it each time so he can perform better against it.

One common fear is getting winded so badly that you can't breathe. First, we engage this fear by talking about it. Next, we devise tactics for coping. When the solar plexus gets hit hard the diaphragm spasms and 'forgets' how to breathe. So we adopted a common medical technique for panic attacks: blowing into an imaginary paper bag. It works by reminding the body what to do (another example of visualisation).

However talking about paper bags and visualising them isn't enough. It's all theory and no practice. So like everything in karate, we must drill until the response comes naturally.

We begin by recreating the problem. After a hard sprint and a full minute on the pads, I get the fighter to inhale and give his solar plexus a sharp tap. Now he must 'blow' into the bag. Next week, the tap becomes a rap, which becomes a jab, which becomes a punch. We add evasive movement to give the fighter time to 'blow'. Like a boxer who's been hurt, he can either back-pedal or clinch-up until he gets his wind back.

You might be surprised that after all this preparation, no fighter ever needed to do this. That's not the point. We acknowledged the fear, we talked about it, we faced it and we dealt with it. In the end it went away and never happened.

Overcoming these nasty little fears and phobias is important because they tend to be the things that keep you awake at night. You've accepted the test, the line-up, the thirty fights, the big dragon. It's those annoying little 'what ifs' that are really troubling you. Getting these little dragons under control helps to build confidence in the run up to the big day.

Spirit: The Way

Generally I stick to a tangible definition of spirit as emotion and feelings. However the philosophical and religious aspects of spirit are also worth considering in preparing for the Thirty Man Kumite.

Karate is – rightly or wrongly – linked to Zen, which is (almost by definition) intangible and hard to define. Pure Zen is somewhere between a religion and a philosophy with many different schools. Some use meditation, others use chanting or mind-bending puzzles to tease out the deeper meaning of Zen and bring enlightenment. But Zen can also be found in activities as diverse as archery and swordsmanship to flower arranging and tea-making.

There's no obvious connection between these activities. The thing that unites them is not what is done, but rather the way it's done. In short, it's the approach that counts.

What is the right approach? Whatever you're doing, at work, in art or in life, certain things are always helpful. Being present in the moment. Attentive to what's happening. Undistracted. Open. Mindful. Calm. Alert. Aware. In karate, this approach helps you train most effectively. In kumite, it helps you see what's happening. Not just the obvious (Yang) but also the less obvious

(Yin) – so you see the big picture, the Tao, the whole. This 'seeing' allows you to take the right action. It gives you all the facts you need to judge correctly. This simultaneous act of seeing and acting is akin to riding a bike. The small nuances of the road mean we're constantly making adjustments to remain on balance, taking in information and making judgements as we go. There's no fixed path, no right or wrong, no single way to ride a bike. This constant balancing act has the feeling of something ever changing and always moving. In karate, and in Zen, this is 'Do' – the Way.

Training for the Thirty Man takes a good deal of judgement and maturity. Your preparation will take extra time out of your day. It'll take your mental focus too. As the test approaches, it'll occupy your every waking moment. So it's important to consider how this will affect those around you, your partner, family, friends, and your work or studies.

As a rule of thumb, take the extra training time out of your own time, not your partner's or your family's. Use early mornings before the rest are awake. Go to bed an hour earlier to catch up on your sleep. If you have kids, do more with them to make up for it. Keeping the support of your nearest and dearest is very worthwhile. It's hard to focus on training if you've just had a row at home. Far better is to know you have love and support behind you.

Aim to train happy. It may seem like a stretch, but if you can enjoy your training, you'll be drawn to it. If you hate it, you'll shy away from it. Find ways to have fun. Train with people you like. Enjoy the feeling of getting stronger, fitter and mentally tougher. Be playful in sparring. Use humour to dispel tension. One of the most memorable performances of recent years for me was the Bristol fighter, Simon Mackown, who was laughing and joking in between thirty hard-fought fights. Enjoying his experience, he was drawn to it and even seemed to thrive on it. Fighting him at the very end, I remember him striking hard and being difficult to hit, which must have made him even happier.

Fighting Spirit

Much is made of the importance of fighting spirit in kumite, and rightly so. It's the biggest factor by far in performance. Over the years in DKK, I've seen some strong fit guys drop out of gradings and some fairly unfit people pass by sheer will alone. Can this spirit, this willpower, be trained? A few years ago I might have said it was innate and you either have it or you don't. But recently one of the fighters I coached proved me wrong and now I believe it can be cultivated and grown.

Most of the candidates I'd coached in the past had been tempered by ten tough DKK gradings up to black belt. However Juha Makinen had cross-graded to black belt from another style. Technically he was excellent, with crisp kihon, good footwork and high kicks that whipped

up and back before you could blink. At around six foot
and eighty-five kilos, he was also a big strong boy and
he'd performed strongly in his gradings for shodan-ho
(probationary black belt) and shodan. However when it
came to his Five Man Kumite in January, he suffered
badly and got put on the floor by body-shots many times.
After, I asked if he had a broken rib and he told me his
ribs were fine. This gave me cause for concern.

When we began training together, I was pleased to see
that despite being forty-six, Juha's fitness was good. He
was training independently and his fitness was growing
each week. He picked up the drills quickly too. But all
this would count for nothing if we couldn't change his
mind-set. We began with never showing tiredness during
training, which he managed easily enough. Next we
waited until his fitness had picked up before adding more
intense mindset exercises. He needed to feel things had
changed since his painful Five Man line-up. We began an
exercise I called the 'Fuck You' drill. He would step
forward in a Sanchin stance and I'd hit him four times.
He'd take the blows unanswered and then step forward,
up in my face, and shove me away hard. I wanted him to
shout, 'Fuck You!' at the same time, but he was too polite
for that. Never mind – the shove was working nicely.
We'd repeat the drill ten times after each round to embed
the new response. It was the best way I could think of to
develop a new reaction to being stuck, focusing outwards
on his aggressor, rather than inwards on the pain.

As always, I began light. The purpose of the exercise was

less about overcoming pain and more about imprinting a new mindset. The strikes got heavier each week. Soon we dropped the shove and Juha would simply step forward and get hit again. By the end of our training he was taking strikes as hard as anyone with no sign of pain or doubt.

Nevertheless, there's a big difference between training – however hard – and the real thing. So when the time came for his test, the walk to the Field of Truth was a nerve-wracking time for me too. There was always the fear that under pressure, the hard coat of varnish we'd built would crack. Once this hard shell is broken and water starts seeping in, it can quickly become a torrent. I prayed the seal would hold.

So it pleased me no end when, after twenty-nine gruelling fights, I faced Juha for his final battle. He'd weathered the storm beautifully. He'd been on the ground – thrown or swept by vicious low kicks – but not once due to a painful shot. He'd been hit by the biggest and the best and he was still kicking and punching hard, and with some beautiful high kicks peppered throughout. Aged forty-six, he did a truly memorable Thirty Man Kumite. Our final fight was simply more of the same and the perfect reward for our hard training together.

In my experience as a coach, this was probably the biggest turnaround on the nidan journey. Outwardly Juha is still the same guy, quiet and unassuming with his quirky Finnish manner, but he's become one of the most respected and feared fighters in the dojo, and in DKK, that's saying something.

This brings to mind the subtle difference between aggression and fighting spirit. Perhaps it's the difference between combat sports and martial arts. A fighter is actively looking for fights. Seeking a way to expend his aggression. A martial artist feels no aggression, however he won't be bullied or put down. Faced with aggression, he rises accordingly. The harder he's pushed, the deeper he digs. This has been my own experience in the martial arts and I see the same thing repeated year after year. The candidates who take on the Thirty Man Kumite are good men and women, courteous, fair, trustworthy – the kind of people you'd want as a friends. Taken to the violent extreme of thirty full-contact bouts, they respond with equal violence. But after the final blows are struck, they're helped off the field by the very people inflicting the damage. They're served with hot sweet tea and given ice packs, helped back to their tents and applauded each time they return, walking gingerly, to the training fields.

Later by the campfire, younger fighters sit beside them and ask questions, seeking to grasp what seems inconceivable. How do you fight thirty people in such ferocious full-contact sparring without quitting? The answer's hard to put into words, specially after the second or third beer. There's something about doing the right training, but that only takes you so far. Desire helps. The DKK nidan is something worth having, worth fighting for. Aggression is rarely the answer. It burns too bright and too short to see you much beyond the first ten fights. After that, only fighting spirit can bring you home.

Senior fighters who've done the test themselves have no such questions. They simply sit and share in the curious mix of pride, relief and humility that comes after, joined in a camaraderie that can't be bought or manufactured, it can only forged in hardship. This shared venture into violence exposes the spirit and we see, often for the first time, who we really are. The results aren't always pretty. There's often mixed feelings and soul-searching to be done. However one lesson is always the same: we are capable of so much more than we thought possible, and for this alone the Thirty Man Kumite is worth the sweat and the hurt.

Summer 2013: Simon Clinch, Ben Hung, Andy Bremerkamp and Ragi McFadden line up

Ragi McFadden (left) with Mei Mei Tang, 2013

Simon Clinch (left) early in the line at Summer Camp 2013

Ben Hung (left) v Dave Urquhart, near the end at Summer 2013

Happy days preparing with Danny Bard in Spring, 2014

Rob Curtis, final fight with me, Dan Lewis officiating, 2014

Juha Makinen evades my kick in the closing seconds, 2014

Crisp new Black Gis: Danny Bard (l) and Juha Makinen (r) with Sensei Gavin, 2014

The Idea of Concepts

Once a fighter is good, it takes a lot more work to get a little bit better. Progress often involves small improvements in movement. As a coach, it can be hard to convey the subtle changes you're looking for. Explaining nuanced movements in words is like trying to sculpt a statue out of bricks.

Rather than using language, it's often better to paint a picture. This brings us back to that most useful of all training tools: visualisation. We've already used basic visualisation like imaginary lines of energy, and pictured the line-up to drop adrenaline. But visualisation can go further, into the realm of concepts. Now, rather than seeing a picture, you're involved in a video, like a 3D simulation. Imagine you're an animal: a tiger, a crane, a snake. Imagine you're firing an arrow at a target. Imagine your feet are buried in thick mud. Imagine there's a current of energy flowing through your body.

The value of concepts was driven home to me about ten years ago when one of our senior students became obsessed with Sanchin, a stance and a kata familiar to students of Goju Ryu and Kyokushinkai. He practised it constantly, seeking the natural power and resilience to strikes it can bring. One evening, frustrated with his inability to grasp the kata, he demanded an explanation of the 'rooting' that's a key element of Sanchin. He asked, quite rightly, how can we be truly rooted since our feet remain above the ground. The only answer I could offer was that 'rooting' was a concept. The locking of the feet on the floor and the sinking of bodyweight are meant to create a sense of rooting into the earth. This was, for him, a light-bulb moment and his study of Sanchin continued more happily. Pretty soon he was demonstrating a natural power and a remarkable ability to take strikes with seemingly no pain whatsoever. It took me a while longer to have my own light-bulb moment: namely that so many controversial ideas in martial arts can be accepted as concepts rather than argued over as a reality. Animal styles are a good example. There's no need to take monkey boxing or crane style too literally. If you watch boxing or MMA you'll see fighters have their own styles. Some are aggressive and ferocious. Some are cold and calculating with surgical strikes. Some are relentless. Some are sneaky and evasive. If we relate these to animal styles you can see how tiger style would be stalking, pouncing and tearing-up. Bear would be a heavy handed mauling. Dog would be relentless. Crane or mantis would be still and waiting, aiming precision blows. Bull would be driving forward. Snake would be tying up and constricting. Once you have a clear picture of these concepts, there's no need to think, 'I must stand still, use less energy, and only react when I see an opening'. All you have to think is 'Mantis'.

You don't have to form your fingers into claws to fight like a tiger or into a beak to fight like a crane (although you can if you like). It's more the style, strategy and movement you're seeking to emulate in your own fighting. Here are some of the most useful concepts to help you in your martial arts training.

Chi – Vital Energy

Almost all traditional martial arts use the concept of Chi in some form. These days Chi is often written as 'Qi', however the old spelling still features in arts like Tai Chi (also written 'Taiji') and Chi Gung (Qigong). In Japanese it is the 'Ki' found in aikido and kiai – the 'spirited shout' that helps to focus energy. Many masters and schools try to prove the existence of Chi as a form of magnetic energy that flows around the earth and through the body. Sceptics – usually Westerners – regard it as hokum designed to attract gullible students and insist only hard training can deliver powerful results. Rather than engage in the debate, I urge you to view Chi as a concept and move on. And if you still want a debate you can ponder, like Plato, whether something that exists only in the mind counts as real?

Real or not, the concept of Chi is incredibly useful in the martial arts. Chi translates loosely as Vital Energy. One of the best ways to picture vital energy is to consider the difference between a living body and a corpse. Imagine a paramedic checking for vital signs – blood-flow, breathing, nervous signals – all these flow through the body, animating it and keeping it alive.

In arts like Chi Gung and Tai Chi the aim is to cultivate a

strong flow of Chi to keep the body healthy. In karate, we build cardio vascular fitness (blood-flow and breathing) and improve reflexes (nervous signals) through the body. Even the idea of 'cultivating' vital energy is useful. It implies a gentle and constant coaxing of health and fitness rather than always pushing as hard as you can and draining the body of energy.

Vital energy waxes and wanes in line with the body's biorhythms. It's important to get in tune with your body's differing cycles that are daily, weekly, monthly and yearly. The start of the day isn't ideal for training because you've just woken up. However early morning is a useful time if you're busy with work or studies. A light-to-medium session is best at this time. Mid-morning is a good time to train hard because breakfast has been digested. Mid-afternoon and early evening are good too. If you're training in the evening, eat a light snack at 4pm and have dinner after. Late night training isn't ideal because the body is easing down for sleep. However if you can only train at unusual times of day, then do so. Adapt your eating habits to fit and your body's biorhythms will re-form around your new regime.

In terms of weekly cycles, there's a reason why the common working week is five days. This is the amount of work we can do before we feel overworked. We all know how, if we work at the weekend, we feel especially cheated of those two days' rest. Training five days a week is the most common recommendation for serious sportspeople. Most of the people I've coached have stuck to it with good results. Six days is possible but I don't recommend it unless you're younger than average (under thirty) and you need to spend extra time on technique.

A typical five day programme might include two days of dojo training in the week and a partner session on Saturday. These would be your three hard sessions. In between would be two solo training sessions, perhaps one cardio and one heavy bag and weights. You'll find your energy levels wax and wane over the week. Try to get a smooth rhythm going so you can make small improvements each week. Make sure your three hard sessions remain hard and adjust your solo sessions until you're improving in your hard sessions each week.

There's often a 'slump week' that seems to follow a monthly cycle. After three good weeks you have a poor week. Treat this slump week as a recovery week by cutting down solo training or taking a couple of extra days' rest. Aim to hit the next week with renewed energy and reach a new plateau.

It's helpful to try and reach a few smaller peaks before scaling the big one in June. This is like an Olympic athlete who takes a few warm-up tournaments, but not too many, before the big games. Work towards a strong Five Man Kumite in January and a good tournament in April to test yourself under pressure. Try to get in tune with your body's natural vital energy and ride the waves, so you reach highpoints at the right times. Keep in mind that to reach higher, you must also be prepared to go lower. That means not being afraid to rest hard in between training and take time off to recover, knowing that it's the only way to come back stronger.

So far we've only explored the biological aspects of Chi. The beauty of Chi is it reaches much further. The idea originated thousands of years before science broke everything down into bite-sized chunks of biology, physics and chemistry. Chi encompasses all of these, as does a fight, and a fighter, so consider it a bundle of scientific phenomena working in unison.

Above all, Chi is about flow. Consider the flow of energy that goes from eating a banana to striking an opponent. Chemistry, biology and physics are all at work. Scientists could write pages about what exactly happened, but that's going into unnecessary detail. All the fighter needs to do is seek the perfect balance of eating, resting and training to maximise this natural flow of energy.

Much of what energises a fighter comes from training right, resting right and eating right. However during combat, there's another energy source that's more important than any of these: breathing. A steady air supply feeds muscles with the oxygen they need to work hard. When you're operating close to your limit, even one missed breath can upset your performance. This isn't a big concern in most sports. A runner can simply breathe in time with his stride. But in kumite, where punches hit the body, you can't take breathing for granted. Your opponent's strikes will disrupt your intake if you're not prepared. Even a light strike on the button of the solar plexus can knock the wind out of you and make you feel sick. Hard shots to the liver and floating ribs can have the same effect. This can cause your diaphragm (the muscle that operates the lungs) to seize up, cutting off your oxygen supply. The feeling of suffocation is like drowning in open air, which in turn leads to panic – none of which is good because you're still in a fight.

The answer is a more sophisticated breath-control first encountered in Sanchin kata: abdominal breathing. Here we visualise drawing breath down into the pit of the stomach rather than raising and expanding the chest. In effect we're educating the diaphragm and lungs to operate down and back rather than up and out, allowing us to keep the outer ab-muscles crunched while breathing inside. I like to think of the solar plexus as a canary bobbing around inside a cage. If you raise and expand the chest you open the cage door and the cat can reach in. If you keep the chest down and the abs crunched, the door remains shut and the cat goes hungry.

Abdominal breathing takes time to develop. Practise Sanchin breathing and rapping on your abs using hammer-fists. Then get a partner to strike your body while you try and breathe inside the cage. Once you can do this, it's time develop more sophisticated breathing rhythms. When you throw combinations, you should be using short, sharp out-breaths in time with your strikes. When your opponent hits your body, you should match his strikes with sharp out-breaths to avoid getting winded. If his strikes are too fast to track, then one sustained out-breath is a good general cover.

So far we've only considered the biological and chemical aspects of Chi. There's plenty of physics at work too. The energy we take in through training, food and air gets transferred, via strikes, from our own body into our opponent's.

It helps to visualise this flow of energy as a ball travelling along a meridian or pathway. The ball comes from the floor, travels up the leg, through the hip-twist, up the torso, through the shoulder-twist, along the arm, out of the fist and into the opponent. Bang! This visualisation helps to develop a natural flow of energy using the entire bodyweight, rather than a set of separate movements. Think of a baseball pitcher winding up for a throw. There's a wave-like flow through his body.

These imaginary meridians don't end in the body. They extend, like laser sight-lines, from your hand to a spot on your target, and beyond. The more you can stay on your trajectory, the smoother the transfer of energy. That means less of your energy is wasted or dissipated, and more of it ends up where you want it: in your opponent.

Yin, Yang and Tao

Yin, Yang and Tao are, like Chi, useful concepts. Tao is the Whole, the Universe, the Big Picture, and like any picture, it's made up of component parts: Yin and Yang. Yang is the thing and Yin is the background or the rest. Yang is hard, visible, tangible. Yin is soft, invisible, intangible. Yin, Yang and Tao are useful frames of reference to make sure we're seeing the big picture. Most of the time, what we're actually seeing is Yang (the thing) rather than Yin and Yang (the thing and the background). When we think of training, we think of the time spent in the dojo or at the gym. However in the bigger picture, recovery is equally important. What we might once have perceived as the opposite of training is in fact an integral part of it.

So consider what are the invisible supporting factors that enable good training? As your training grows in intensity, so must your rest. That might mean going to bed earlier, or dropping activities that don't relate to karate.

What else supports training? Food and hydration come to mind. I don't advocate any special diet, just a balanced one with a good mix of protein, carbs, fruit and veg. I do recommend cutting out sweets, treats and unhealthy snacks. Why make things harder by carrying extra weight?

When you're training hard five days a week, you'll want a healthy breakfast, lunch and dinner and probably some added fuel mid-morning and mid-afternoon. Here's the kind of diet that works for most fighters: porridge, cereal or eggs in the morning. Banana mid-morning. Sandwiches and fruit for lunch. Toast or flapjack at 4pm before evening training. Dinner when you get home – meat or fish with pasta, rice or potatoes and green veg like broccoli or spinach. You get the idea. Sip water throughout the day so you're hydrated before training, as well as during and after. The odd glass of wine or beer won't hurt but do you really need it? Even a slight hangover or a touch of dehydration affects your morning training. You sleep less deeply and wake a little more groggy. This impacts on your recovery. Training for the Thirty Man is hard enough, why make it harder?

Once you reach base camp (eight weeks before the test) I suggest you cut out alcohol completely. More important than any physical reason is the mental knowledge that you've 'eaten bitter' in training. You've deprived yourself. You've suffered for your art and done everything possible to prepare correctly. When you're tired, battered and hanging over the precipice of failure, you can know, absolutely in your heart of hearts, that you did everything right and you deserve to pass. This is what you want going through your head, rather than wishing you hadn't had all those extra pies and pints.

Think of Yin as an enabling force that supports Yang. If Yang is a punch, Yin is the load. If Yang is training, Yin is recovery. If Yang is effort, Yin is relaxation. The more you strip away what is unnecessary, the more you have is stock for what is necessary. Rather than being the opposite, Yin is the other side of the same coin. Only when you consider Yin and Yang together do you really see the big picture, the whole, the Tao.

Martial Principles

As we advance in karate, we begin to see that behind the bewildering array of techniques there are underlying principles at work. A principle is a rule or law that holds good whatever the practice. Once you're familiar with a principle, you can perform a thousand techniques without having to learn each one.

A simple example is what goes up must come down. So if you lift your opponent up, you know he'll be coming down. Now you can plan ahead, and use a sweep or a throw. By the same principle, if his foot is up, it will soon come down. If you can process this knowledge fast enough, you can sweep the foot just before it lands. Or time a low-kick to hit as his foot plants, making it hard for him to block or evade.

Another example is the shortest distance between two bodies is a straight line. So if your opponent leads with circular techniques like hooks, strike in a straight line and hit first. If you wait until you see the hook coming it's probably too late. But by knowing this principle and simply firing straight down the centre line, you stack the odds in your favour.

Similarly, a small circle fits inside a big circle. So if your opponent is throwing big hooks and you're throwing tight hooks, yours should land first. Untrained street brawlers tend to throw wild haymakers that you can see coming for miles. Professional boxers keep their hooks tight and close. They aren't too bothered by what's happening outside shoulder-width. Keeping your techniques tight is like taking the inside track in a race. As long as you're sharp, you should land first.

The importance of principles is often repeated. What's mentioned less frequently is what those principles are. As part of my fifth dan grading I spent some time trying to identify the universal principles of karate.

I began with the premise that they are contained in the kata. The karate masters of Okinawa were consistent in their message that one or two kata, studied deeply, were all that's required to learn how to fight. Since a single kata only contains a handful of techniques, the implication is that it's the principles that teach a fighter to cope in any situation. For example by training the sideways foot-sweep in the first kata, we learn it relies on breaking the opponent's balance and taking away his supporting structure. By following this principle, we can perform any number of other sweeps, front, back, inside, outside, whenever we see an opponent off balance or succeed in breaking his balance.

Now we begin to see the real beauty of kata. Rather than viewing it as a set of suggested techniques, we begin to see it as enacting martial principles. The movements are deliberately formalised to be clear about the principles at work. A forward stance isn't saying your front stance should always look exactly like this. It's saying 'weight is thrown forward in this technique'. Likewise a back stance is saying 'throw your weight back,' and a low horse-riding stance is saying 'drop your weight'.

I began searching for principles in the first kata in our system, Gekisai Dai Ichi. After considering the bow, the preparatory 'Yoi' and the first movement, I was astonished to find a whole raft of principles falling out faster than I could write them down. Equally surprising was that after this, I struggled to find many more.

My list isn't intended to be comprehensive. There may be many more that can be identified. Some are more 'rules of thumb' rather than universal principles and I've included them because I think they're useful. At the end, I've tried to list them in a memorable way for those facing the Thirty Man.

Like every kata, Gekisai Dai Ichi begins with a bow. As the saying goes, 'karate begins and ends with respect'. This is a guideline more than a principle. Proper respect will help your training in a great many ways. Respect your teacher, your training partners, your opponent, and yourself. Listen to what people are saying. Watch what they're doing. Consider how they're feeling. Pay attention to everything, including yourself. Make sure you're pushing yourself hard but also looking after yourself. On top of this, respect the test. Attempting the Thirty Man is no small thing. This isn't a grading where you can spend a couple of weeks getting fit and muddle through. Commit to at least six months of focused kumite training followed by two months of punishing fitness. A year is better. In fact, start as soon as the idea crosses your mind.

After the bow comes the 'Yoi' or ready position. This action symbolises Zanshin – awareness. Eventually, like so much else in karate, the aim is to transcend this momentary awakening of awareness to being aware at all times. I can't stress enough how important it is to remain focused in the Thirty Man. When you're tired and battered your mind will be desperate to switch off and look away. The moment you do this is the moment you get badly hurt. It's always the unexpected blow that takes you out.

The mental strength to stay focused can be cultivated in your regular training. Be the first in the dojo. Be the first in the line-up. Be alert to every command. Hit every position correctly first time. Perform kihon like your life depended on it. Snap out every strike and lock down every stance. Use this form of mental exercise to sharpen your concentration and focus. By the end of each class you should be mentally as well as physically exhausted. However like all training, the more you do it, the more it comes naturally. Then your alertness can stay on a razor's edge while your mind remains calm.

Another aspect of 'Yoi' is a sense of commitment. This is a recurring theme in karate and never more so than in the Thirty Man. Commitment begins with the right training early on and takes you through to the test itself. Like many things, it can be cultivated. As well as sticking to your training regime, try to bring commitment into your everyday thought, speech and action. Avoid half-heartedness and indecision of any kind. You're either training or you're resting. You're either injured or you're not. You either want a pickle in your burger or you don't.

When talking with other karate-ka, and even with your sensei, be clear and positive. That includes being clear about what you can't do. If you can't spar, say so and don't change your mind. If you can't train, don't train. Go home and rest. If you can spar, but you have a sprained finger, strap it up, wear a glove and tell your opponent. Then spar. Be decisive. Take responsibility for your progress and your health. Assert your will and take control. In the end, the ability to push through the Thirty Man Kumite is an act of commitment. Be bloody-minded about it and simply decide to do it.

The first step in Gekisai Dai Ichi is an important one because it enacts a key tactic – stepping off the line of attack. Your opponent is using a text-book attack – a straight punch down the centre-line. He's following a principle we've already identified, namely the shortest distance between two bodies is a straight line. Since he started first, you can't expect to beat him to the punch. So the onus is on you to move off the line of attack. That's what this step represents. This fighting over lines and angles brings us to arguably the most useful strategic principle of all: fight for positional advantage.

Getting a better position is as useful in stand-up as it is on the ground. It holds true for one against one, one against many and army against army. It's a principle I return to time and again in coaching. Let it be your guiding principle at all times. Any time you can attack from the side or rear, grab the chance. Do this by forcing your opponent off the centre-line, repositioning yourself at an angle, or both. These skills really come to the fore in the second, more advanced version of the kata, Gekisai Dai Ni. To keep things simple, I include several smaller principles under this big one:

- Control the centre-line if you can, forcing him to go around
- Control distance so you're fighting at a range that suits you
- Take the inside track using tight circles rather than open swings
- Use gravity by getting on top or fighting from uphill
- Time your attacks to land when he's not in a position to defend

Returning to the kata – as we step we sink, turn and rise, rotating as we do, to fire out the upper block. This action throws bodyweight into the block. Every technique in every kata should have bodyweight behind it. As a rule of thumb, the body performs the action momentarily before the limb, creating torque and firing the limb more powerfully. There are several ways to throw bodyweight: forwards and backwards, up and down, rotating left and right, even a sharp compression of the core. These are evident in the stances of the kata, which are deliberately stylised to make this clear.

Good body mechanics obey the laws of physics, first outlined by Isaac Newton in his monumental work, called (appropriately) *Principia*. Like all truly great ideas,

Newton's Laws of Motion are simple:

1. Every object continues in its state of rest or uniform motion in a straight line, unless external forces act on it
2. Force = mass x acceleration
3. When two bodies collide, the action and reaction forces are equal but opposite

The first law tells us a punch will continue to fly unless something stops it, like hitting the target or coming to the end of your reach. Either way, it will spring back. The thing to pick up here is how you can harness this natural continuation of momentum. This principle is enacted nicely in the ninth movement of the Gekisasi kata, where an elbow strike becomes a back-fist strike, which flows into a lower block, which flows into a reverse punch. Once you've initiated movement, don't stop. Try to maintain momentum by flowing from one technique to the next.

Newton's second law, force = mass x acceleration, is often cited as a way to measure the force of a punch, however it only relates to the body throwing the punch. When it comes to impact – the transfer of energy from one body to another – we need the equation for kinetic energy which, in Newtonian mechanics, is:

$E(k) = \frac{1}{2}mv^2$ (or: kinetic energy = mass x velocity$^2 \div 2$)

From this we see speed (v) makes more difference than mass (m) because the value for speed is squared. So while throwing bodyweight into a technique makes a difference, speed makes a far greater difference. You only have to consider the mass of a bullet to see it's speed that kills.

Newton's third law says action and reaction are the same. The greater the impact on your opponent, the greater the impact on you. So it's important to strike from a firm base and tense on impact. That way your opponent feels the effect of the impact more than you do.

Here I've tried to condense these principles into a useful and memorable format:

- Show respect to others, to yourself, and to the test
- Cultivate awareness and focus in everything you do
- Fight for positional advantage using distance, timing and angles
- Throw bodyweight into each technique
- Being fast makes more difference than being big
- Maintain flow for maximum efficiency
- Cultivate a spirit of commitment in all your actions

Don't misunderstand this spirit of commitment as believing you're always right. If you have a question or concern, ask your coach or your sensei. But otherwise, maintain a mind-set of quiet commitment and get out of the habit of wavering.

The Art of War

All warfare is based on deception. When able to attack, we must seem unable. When we are near, we must make the enemy believe we are far away. When far away, we must make him believe we are near. Hold out baits to entice the enemy. Feign disorder and crush him.

I love this stuff, don't you? It's what elevates fighting to what the boxer Lennox Lewis called 'chess with muscles'. Recently I've encouraged candidates to read Sun Tzu's Art of War and highlight passages that apply to them. Strategy is always useful and never more so than for the Thirty Man. There are plenty of books out there, including samurai and western military strategy, but the genius of Sun Tzu is how simply and eloquently he states things. The writing can be a little enigmatic at times, but easy enough to follow once you get the hang of it.

The treatise is written for armies, but it applies equally in single combat. Think of the army as a human body comprised of mind, body and spirit. Mind is the general, body is the men, spirit is morale. I've focused on strategies for a smaller force facing larger force, since this has the most relevance to the Thirty Man Kumite.

If he is in superior strength, evade him.

The Thirty Man Kumite puts even the strongest, most talented fighter at a disadvantage. If you're a good fighter, this is something you might rarely have experienced. Be prepared to adapt your training and use strategies you might not usually employ. Ego must be set aside. Learn to think like a smaller, smarter fighter.

Attack him where he is unprepared, appear where you are not expected.

Practise controlling distance, timing and angles to land your attacks. Use movement that suggests you're going backwards before going forwards. Take your opponent off the centre-line and attack from the side.

Let your great object be victory, not lengthy campaigns.

Your objective is a strong performance all the way to the end. So while you must attack every fighter, don't get bogged down in wars of attrition. Don't allow any single fighter to knock you off your rhythm. Be like a ship going through a storm. Set your course into the waves and allow them to crash over you as you make your way steadily through.

The clever combatant imposes his will on the enemy, but does not allow the enemy's will to be imposed on him.

Set a pace that you know, from training, you can hold to the end. Don't let fierce fighters make you go crazy. Respond to surges but only up to a point. Otherwise, think like an experienced runner and stay on the pace. Don't try to conserve too much energy either because it's hard to make up lost ground. Control the pace and control the race.

If you know the enemy and know yourself, you need not fear the result of a hundred battles.

One of Sun Tzu's most famous quotes, and for good reason. Know your enemy. Study as many fighters as you can. Spar with them often so their style becomes familiar. Prepare for the kinds of attacks you know will come. There aren't all that many, but they'll come hard and fast so you must prepare deeply.

The good fighters of old first put themselves beyond the possibility of defeat, and then waited for an opportunity of defeating the enemy.

Prepare for hundreds of hard attacks: straight punches, front-kicks, low kicks, round kicks, hooks and uppercuts. Knees and grabs. Learn to deal with them under pressure. Train to strike hard for thirty minutes. Put yourself beyond the possibilities of defeat. Then look for your opponent's openings... and attack.

To secure ourselves against defeat lies in our own hands, but the opportunity of defeating the enemy is provided by the enemy himself.

Securing yourself against defeat lies in doing the right training, outlined above. Train so whichever attack your opponent uses, you're drilled to respond instantly and strike back.

Standing on the defensive indicates insufficient strength; attacking, a superabundance of strength.

I don't recommend a defensive mindset but neither do I suggest chasing after your opponent. It's his job to give you a hard fight. If he doesn't, then hit him by all means, but remember you don't look good beating on a weak fighter. You look a lot better raising your game against a strong one.

Making no mistakes is what establishes the certainty of victory. Hence the skilful fighter puts himself into a position that makes defeat impossible, and does not miss the moment for defeating the enemy.

Train attack and defence drills so you can read every attack and react instantly. With my most skilful fighters, I would throw a mix of front and round kicks – left or right, front or back foot – and they would read eight or nine out of every ten correctly. This ability to read puts you beyond the surprise attacks and unforeseen strikes that do the most damage.

In all fighting the direct method may be used for joining battle, but indirect methods will be needed in order to secure victory.

Direct methods are Yang, stepping forwards and striking. Indirect methods are Yin, evasion and redirection. Without Yin, you are setting yourself up for a head-to-head test of strength that you're unlikely to win.

Indirect tactics, efficiently applied, are inexhaustible as Heaven and Earth, unending as the flow of rivers and streams. Like the sun and moon, they end but to begin anew, and like the four seasons, they pass away to return once more.

The softness and flow of parries, evasion and blending take less effort and put you in good positions from which to strike back hard.

In battle there are not more than two methods of attack – the direct and the indirect, yet these two in combination give rise to an endless series of manoeuvres. The direct and the indirect lead onto each other in turn. It is like moving in a circle – you never come to an end. Who can exhaust the possibilities of their combination?

Flowing from soft to hard, from evasion to counter-strike, must happen naturally. Interspersing hard movement with soft allows you to breathe deeply, relieve tension and renew energy so you can strike hard once more.

There are not more than five musical notes, yet the combinations of these five give rise to more melodies than can ever be heard.

There are not more than five primary colours (blue, yellow, red, white, and black) yet in combination they produce more hues than can ever been seen.

There are not more than five cardinal tastes (sour, acrid, salt, sweet, bitter) yet combinations of them yield more flavours than can ever be tasted.

Imagine five primary attacks: straight punches, front kicks, round kicks, round punches and knees. There will be subtle variations of angle with each fighter, but close enough that you only need to train for these five attacks. They can come in an infinite variety of combinations, but fundamentally there are only five to work on. Get to know them well.

The good fighter will be terrible in his onset and prompt in his decision.

You must be careful not to waste energy, so any attack you make must be instant and committed.

All armies prefer high ground to low ground and sunny places to dark.

Train your footwork to naturally seek a positional advantage. If there is a slope (as there is on the Field of Truth) then work to keep the higher ground but never look down or around. Focus resolutely on your opponent. Don't worry about sunshine or shade. Keep looking at your opponent and if the sun's in your eyes, squint.

If the enemy leaves a door open, you must rush in.

Ignore obvious traps but if you see an opening, take it. Punish openings without hesitation, otherwise you're forced to attack heavily guarded positions.

Forestall your opponent by seizing what he holds dear.

Disrupt your opponent's rhythm by attacking just before his big attack. It needn't be a big effort, just enough to make him reconsider.

At first, exhibit the coyness of a maiden, until the enemy gives you an opening.

There are no coy maidens on the Field of Truth. The idea is not to give your opponent what he wants. If he invites you in to get up close and personal, keep away. Then pay him a visit when he's not expecting you.

Move not unless you see an advantage. Use not your troops unless there is something to be gained. Fight not unless the position is critical.

You can't afford to waste energy, so move only when necessary. Be on the lookout for moments when a strike will definitely connect, then be decisive so it counts.

The clever combatant looks to the effect of combined energy and does not require too much from individuals. Hence his ability to pick out the right men and utilise combined energy.

The total fighter is a combination of things. Rather than using pure strength, or pure speed, he combines them in the right way. If he finds himself out of breath he clinches up to recover. If he feels himself taking too much punishment he gets on his toes and dances away. If his left leg takes a pounding, he puts his right leg forward until the left recovers, taking energy from one tank while the other refills.

When he utilises combined energy, his fighting men become as it were like unto rolling logs or stones. The energy developed by good fighting men is as the momentum of a round stone rolled down a mountain thousands of feet in height.

Try and develop rolling energy on two levels. Physically,

keep a flow of rotational momentum across the shoulders and hips in basics and pad-work. Tactically, try and flow between several ways of fighting. Work from outside, then from striking distance, then at close-range. Vary your defences between blocks, evasions and disruptions. Avoid being stiff and predictable.

Regard your soldiers as your children, and they will follow you into the deepest valleys; look upon them as your own beloved sons, and they will stand by you even unto death.

The general takes care of his men and this builds morale. Take care of your body. Don't take unnecessary punishment to prove a point. Concentrate on inflicting it instead.

Carefully study the wellbeing of your men and do not overtax them. Concentrate your energy and hoard your strength. Keep your army continually on the move and devise unfathomable plans.

In training and in fighting, you're looking to inflict maximum impact on your opponent with minimal impact on yourself. Be bold but not reckless. You can't hurt your opponent properly if you're taking punishment yourself.

Throw your soldiers into positions whence there is no escape and they will prefer death to flight. If they will face death, there is nothing they may not achieve. Officers and men alike will put forth their uttermost strength.

Don't mistake this for recklessness. This is a call for total commitment. The samurai who has accepted death is free to fight without fear. Facing the Thirty Man Kumite you aren't going to die, but you are going to get hit, get hurt, and get taken to your limit. Accept this up front and move on. Decide to finish, no matter what. Give yourself no opt-out clause. Then you don't have to keep contending with niggling doubts and negative voices. In my own test, I decided the only way I'd fail was if I was carried off on a stretcher... and there was no stretcher in the dojo. This mind-set got me through my darkest moments.

Place your army in deadly peril and it will survive. Plunge it into desperate straits and it will come off in safety.

Cultivate the mind-set of 'finishing no matter what'. Commitment is your best path to safety. Wavering is a slippery slope you don't want to find yourself on.

Be stern in the council chamber so that you may control the situation.

In the final week of coaching, I tell my fighters I'm handing over the reins. They're in control and responsible for their own fate. I encourage them to be decisive in their manner with everyone – friends and family, even the chief instructors. Show no doubt. Allow no doubt in.

What enables the good general to strike and conquer and achieve things beyond the reach of ordinary men is foreknowledge. This cannot be elicited from spirits. It cannot be obtained inductively from experience, nor by any deductive calculation. Knowledge of the enemy's dispositions can only be obtained from other men – hence the use of spies.

'The Use of Spies' is the final chapter in The Art of War and it's clear Sun Tzu considers it the most important of all. Quite simply, a general is unable to formulate any strategies or plans without knowledge of the enemy. Military intelligence, both then and now, is the most valuable weapon in the general's arsenal. In the Thirty Man Kumite, your most vital skill is the ability to read your opponent's intentions. This foreknowledge of incoming strikes buys you precious time to react when you're tired and ensures you're never taken by surprise.

The end and aim of spying in all its varieties is knowledge of the enemy.

Learning to read attacks takes time. Build the skill slowly with a partner by drilling reactions to pre-defined 'telegraphed' attacks. Gradually reduce the prescription and the telegraphing. Aim to read eight out of every ten kicks correctly. If you're falling short of this, make the drill easier again.

It is only the enlightened ruler and the wise general who will use the highest intelligence of the army for purposes of spying and thereby they achieve great results.

Invest time in learning to read your opponent. Then invest more time in learning to read your opponent. It will never be time wasted.

Whether or not you plan to face the Thirty Man Kumite, I suggest you read and re-read the Art of War every few years. You'll refresh your existing knowledge and discover new depths each time you do.

Peak Performance

In the long build up to the test you've had the luxury of time to develop strategy, tactics, technique and mindset. You've built your fitness steadily, along with your reaction speed, focus and commitment. This period of walking in the foothills has given you time to get everything in place, but now those carefree days are over. Eight weeks before the test you're at Everest Base Camp, so take a couple of extra days' rest because from here onwards the climb is steep and hard.

You might need to adjust your schedule. Dojo sessions that used to be tough won't trouble you now thanks to your new fitness. So dial up your solo and partner training, and set one as a 'barometer' session to measure your progress. The weekend is good for this because the test happens at the weekend and your body will be used to peaking at this time. Be prepared to adjust other sessions so you can put more into your barometer session.

How you train should also change subtly. Up to now you should have been doing hard sparring at every opportunity. Now you should still spar, but try and avoid long grinding sessions that risk injuries. Choose your sparring partners wisely and keep things crisp and contained. Avoid the temptation to spar softly because you tend to pick up injuries you'd never get if you were taking things more seriously. In the last few weeks, tail off with the sparring and concentrate on dialling up the intensity on the pads.

Over the last eight weeks the aim is to extend your intensity a little more each week. Begin with twenty minutes of cardio-based exercises to warm up: footwork drills, kihon and partner drills. Then kick things off hard with six hard sprints to fire things up and hit some hard one-minute rounds on the pads. In week one, set a goal of fifteen rounds, with two 2-minute breaks in between. Work towards increasing these sets gradually each week, until you do thirty hard rounds in the final week. While concentrating on pad-work, include sprints, burpees and (towards the end of the session) body-conditioning to replicate the challenges of the test.

Whatever you can do over fifteen rounds in week one is

what you aim to do over thirty rounds by week eight. If you can also improve your intensity each week that's great, but the aim is to extend what you have. That's why it's so important to reach base camp in great shape.

During this eight-week period there are some important things to bear in mind. You'll never feel good about your training. You'll always feel a little tired and worn by the intensity and the growing nerves. As soon as you feel any freshness, it'll get used up in another hard session. By now you know your own body, and your own mind, so be prepared to take an extra day's rest if you need it. Just make sure you hit your barometer session hard so you can feel progress each week. From fifteen rounds to eighteen rounds, to twenty rounds, to twenty-five rock-solid hard-hitting rounds. Avoid the temptation to do thirty rounds each time. Start with fifteen but make them ferocious.

While you're giving each round your all, don't let it show. Keep your effort masked. If your opponent sees you trying really hard, he knows you're at the edge and one extra push will tip you over. Don't give him that knowledge. It goes back to the idea of 'cold' mentioned earlier. Ironically, by shaving a little off your effort and redirecting it into your focus, your power will improve. It's something I feel when holding the pads. More of your attention is directed 'outwards' into hurting your opponent, rather than inwards, into how hard you're trying. Where the mind leads the body follows and this external focus adds intent to your striking.

In truth you can't do thirty rounds at 100 percent effort.

You can't even do fifteen rounds at 100 percent effort. The Thirty Man Kumite is closer to a 10K run than a sprint. If you watch the top middle distance runners they're running hard but not flat out. I tell fighters to aim for around 85 percent of effort level – an arbitrary figure to give them a guideline. At this pace you're working in the higher register of your performance, however you still have something left to give if you need it. If you're facing a truly dangerous fighter you can step it up to 95 percent to protect yourself from damage. Don't give 100 percent because you lose focus and it'll be used against you. Save that last five percent so you know you're in control. Your fighting will be all the better for it.

If you're facing someone who really isn't troubling you, then ease down to 75 percent and conserve fuel. You're still operating in the top quartile of your performance level and don't drop below this figure. It's a grading after all, and you must perform at your best. Too little and the fight won't count – you'll have to fight again.

The irony is that by keeping control of your effort, by being your own boss, by not allowing your opponent to make you over-commit and go into the red, you deliver a performance that's 100 percent the best it can be.

After eight weeks of training that grows in intensity, duration and commitment each week, it's time for your final barometer session. Do thirty killer one-minute rounds just to prove you can do it. Then sleep easy at night. Almost.

Take the last week very easy. Dojo sessions will be light, so try and attend. It's good to stay in touch and feel connected. Absorb the strength of the dojo. It's your dojo, a place you belong, a place you helped to create. The rest of the time do some gentle stretching, a little kata or better still do absolutely nothing at all. There are two days of hard training before the Thirty Man and you'll be very glad of the extra freshness.

The Zone

When is a fighter ready for the Thirty Man? When he's at home in the Zone. What is the Zone? The Zone is where technique is sharp, the pace is ferocious and the mind is calm. This can only be achieved by going into the Zone regularly, and staying a little longer each time. You need to feel power, aggression and focus working together so naturally that it's no big deal. Only then can your mind stop trying so hard and relax and take everything in.

I recall a scene from Top Gear a few years ago, before Jeremy Clarkson threw his weight around one too many times. They had a new coupé with some ridiculously high horsepower and Jeremy was screeching (louder than the tyres) about how it was bonkers and impossible to control. Later in the show they gave the car to Lewis Hamilton, who slouched in the driver's seat like a boy-racer and, using just the palm of one hand, took off and did donuts with a cheesy grin on his face. The difference was that Lewis Hamilton drives faster cars every day of the week. His mind was unperturbed by the power beneath him so he could relax and enjoy himself.

This state of mind can only come from familiarity. So get familiar with the Zone. Step on the gas. Get aggressive. But don't see red, or lose focus. Be alert to what you're doing. Enjoy it. Stay in the Zone as long as you can and as soon as you lose form, stop. Don't carry on training outside the Zone because that's like going back to a family saloon, and you don't drive that way any more.

In the final few weeks before the test, I sometimes find fighters are so fit that they seem tireless. I get the sense they could stay in the Zone for as long as I want and they'll always produce another decent round. I try not to get carried away and instead, stick to the programme. I don't want them to peak before the event. Fifteen minutes was good. Twenty minutes even better. Twenty-five minutes is great. Strictly speaking, thirty rounds in the final week is too much because we should save that for the test, but there's a psychological benefit to knowing you can do them. Either way, don't go over thirty minutes in the Zone. Instead, channel any leftover energy into your next session and step up the intensity: more sprints, more burpees, harder punches, sharper kicks. This is the way to cope with the shocking pace of each fight.

By now the fighter who was unfit, untidy and nervous as hell is so conditioned to hard training that it's become second nature. He has the thousand-yard stare of a veteran and he's so used to being in the Zone that it's no big deal any more. In fact, he's even just a tiny bit bored and itching to get the test done. Now he's ready.

Summer Camp

Eight months ago, seven people lined up in a bar in Epping Forest and announced their intention to attempt the Thirty Man Kumite. It's a testament to the severity of the training that today, as we step onto the Field of Truth, only four are waiting to face their line-up. The others were forced to pull out due to injuries and on medical advice. There is regret in this but no shame. This isn't a test you can attempt unless you're fully fit. Some may try again next year. Others may decide that due to age or chronic injuries, they simply can't attempt this test. As the DKK association matures a new path to nidan has opened for members who, with good reason, can't risk the physical damage.

Looking at the four who line up now, I can only imagine the thoughts running through their heads. They appear calm and focused. If they've been training right, they will have played this awesome moment over in their heads countless times. The sight of the line-up should feel familiar, a homecoming of sorts and a welcome end to the tension that's been building over the year. The climb has been long and arduous. The final assault will be short by comparison but infinitely more brutal. Hopefully they can see past the summit to the blue sky beyond. In less than an hour they can put their fears to rest, one way or another, and this will be a welcome moment. Two of the four are from London, Mike Thornton and Jake Hoban. They've both been training with me and I'm confident they're ready.

I've been coaching Jake for a whole year, literally since last summer camp when he requested the test. In truth his progress has been slow and, at times, hard. Week after week I set him exercises, footwork drills, punching drills, kihon-ido (moving basics). He practised them diligently but each time I saw him, I wasn't happy. I had to correct a seemingly endless stream of issues: distance, technique, focus, balance. As one thing got better, another seemed to regress. Yet Jake had qualities I admired very deeply. His basic fitness was good. He was self-motivated and pushed himself hard at the gym and on the heavy bag. While soft-spoken and warm-hearted, he'd always shown strong spirit in the past and I had little doubt about his resolve. Best of all, Jake was patient, and willing to accept my seemingly constant criticism with good grace.

Mike was different. A big, strong kiwi, tough and affable, he had solid basics and heavy hands. Mike really needed to develop his speed and footwork. Mike's extra training didn't really kick in until January, when the wake-up call of a brutal Five Man Kumite galvanised him into action. In some ways I'm more confident in Mike because he's an experienced fighter who'd been around the block a few times. He came from a tough New Zealand style of karate and taekwondo which gave him some lovely high kicks that come as a surprise from such a solid guy. Mike has made good progress since January but the pressures of work and family have made it difficult for him to train as consistently as I'd have liked.

The other two fighters on the field are from Bristol, Matt Savigear, and the only woman in the line up, Philippa Lovegrove. My impression is they've trained hard and they look ready, although I know Matt is worried about his knees holding out in the test.

Philippa and Jake are called out first. With a short bow to their lines and to the chief instructors, their fights begin. Jake settles quickly into a pattern of long range punches and steady footwork. This is good. If he can hold this pace to the end, he'll do just fine. Philippa seems steady and determined. Things are looking good for both of them. But soon Jake is among the brown belts and this year they're a particularly lethal bunch.

One after another lightning-fast fighter hacks away at his legs and fires stinging shots to the body. In contrast, a heavyweight brown belt from Bristol steps out to continue the assault. He's done well in two recent Kyokushin knockdown tournaments and he fires thundering shots with tremendous power. Jake weathers that storm too and reaches his tenth fight in decent shape. Looking across to Philippa, she appears a little flushed but otherwise unscathed.

After a two minute break the fighting starts again and Matt begins his line-up. He's considerably smaller than

Jake or Mike, so I'm pleased to see he's using good footwork and seems to have a natural fighting savvy. However by the eighth fight, the speed of the brown belts catches up with him. A withering barrage of low kicks sends Matt to the ground. He can't put weight on his badly swollen knee and he's forced to withdraw. His brave attempt has ended, at least for now.

After another two minute break, it's Mike's turn to join the fray. He's been chomping at the bit to get stuck in. It's hard watching the others moving along ahead of you while you're still waiting. Mike begins very strongly and easily holds his own against the early fighters. He does well against the brown belts but by the ninth and tenth fight he seems to tire suddenly. His early enthusiasm has taken its toll and he sustains some heavy punishment.

After the next break, Jake and Philippa are in the final part of their lines. Philippa looks exactly as she did when she started. She's set a steady rhythm and work-rate and fought with complete determination from start to finish. It's a performance to be proud of and as a mother approaching the big 4-0, an inspiration to the younger women in the association.

Jake doesn't look quite so together. In his last five fights his gi is hanging loose and his belt is undone. His eyes are still locked onto his opponents – as we trained so hard to do – but he seems miles away. Several times he gets knocked down by the force of the attacks. He's among the highest grades and the most dangerous fighters. There's little else to do but hang on. Yet that's exactly what he does, getting back to his feet and throwing punches when he can. His accuracy – which has improved dramatically over the year – is shaky now and his punches are going wild. Several people have taken shots in the face, one hard enough to knock him down. Gum-shields are mandatory but I don't like them and sometimes leave mine out. Not this time. I pop it in and notice the fighters beside me doing the same.

When my fight is called, I hold my guard high and search for a safe way to attack. Realising there isn't one, I bite down on my gum-shield and step in. Sure enough I take a few replies in the face, but I'm expecting them and they're not hard enough to deter me. Jake is tall and awkward to fight, his movements are unexpected and unpredictable. I find it hard to catch him cleanly and that, I suppose, is good for him. We've worked long and hard to make his movements more natural and flowing and he's reaped the rewards, but now his old style is serving him equally well.

After a minute of hard fighting, time is called and Jake has finished. He steadies himself with his hands on someone's shoulders as his belt gets retied for him. He's staring into the sky, as if trying to get to grips with the enormity of what he's just accomplished.

Talking briefly after the fight, Jake confesses to being disappointed with his performance. He feels he lost his way towards the end. I reassure him I have no such worries. I'm very happy with the way he fought and impressed with how he finished, standing tall and firing back, even if it was a bit haphazardly! Against a line-up of this calibre, it was quite a feat.

With Philippa and Jake's lines done and Matt out through injury, all attention is on Mike. His lively performance in the first ten fights has taken its toll and by fight fifteen he's slowed down considerably. Nevertheless he fights solidly up to fight twenty and gets a much needed break.

He starts his last ten fights with a little more freshness but by the last five fights, it's clear his energy is spent. This is a horrible position to be in because these are the most fearsome strikers of all. Mike's running on empty with nothing but an iron resolve to finish. He gets knocked down time and again, but gets up one more time than he goes down, weathering five ferocious fights by will alone. For this he deserves, and gets, respect.

Talking to him afterwards, I reassure him his heart and spirit had been strong, and his fighting ability had been clearly on show. In the end, I felt his fitness had been a little lacking, in particular the specific fitness you can only get from dojo sparring and regular work on the heavy bag. Mike seemed to accept this and I hope he'll wear his black gi with the pride it deserves.

Pride, however, is a rare emotion for those who complete the test. Few of us are happy with our performance. Most of us think we could have done better in some way. We feel raw and exposed. The test has shown us who we really are, where our limits lie, and in public, too. We've been taken far beyond our comfort zone to a place we couldn't have imagined six months earlier – a place we'd rather not visit again. Still it's good to know that when we were pushed this far, we might have bent, but we didn't break.

The long climb up the mountain has been an equally deep inner journey. We've encountered a side of ourselves that we rarely meet, that unseen primal mind lurking beneath, controlling so many of our actions. We've seen how it's capable of small acts of cowardice and great acts of courage, and forged a closer working relationship with this essential side of ourselves.

This new understanding of mind, body and spirit represent a huge advance on the path or Way of karate – a journey of self-knowledge that can, and should, last a lifetime.

Philippa Lovegrove, (r) v Mizuki Murai, 2015

Philippa's line includes Darren Heywood, 2015

Jake Hoban under pressure from Andy Bremerkamp, 2015

Jake Hoban (r) v Simon Clinch, Summer 2015

Jake and Philippa, hard pressed on all sides, Summer 2015

Mike Thornton (r) v Ed Barbor, Summer 2015

Mike Thornton looking determined against Darren Heywood

Newly certified nidans with me, Dan Lewis, Jake Hoban, Philippa Lovegrove, Mike Thornton and Gavin Mulholland

Epilogue

At the time of writing, I know of four martial artists, friends and acquaintances, with cancer. Faced with such a test the Thirty Man Kumite pales into insignificance. Theirs is a battle on a whole new level. Speaking to one who'd recently undergone chemo, I was humbled to hear how, when he could barely summon the strength to get out of bed, it was the DKK badge tattooed on his shoulder that got him to his feet. Another is still organising martial arts events despite his illness. Yet another, I see, continues to teach and train in karate. This really is inspiring stuff.

Can the martial arts give us strength in such testing times? I have to believe they can. However, I don't like calling a serious illness a 'battle'. If illness is a battle that can be won or lost, then life itself is a similar battle, with only one eventual outcome. Rather than thinking in terms of winning and losing, I prefer to return to the concept of 'Do' or the Way. What matters is how we approach life and everything it throws at us. How do we engage with the life we have? How do we go about reaching goals and avoiding obstacles? Can we do it without trampling over the people we meet on the way? How do we treat the ones we should love and cherish the most? How do we deal with people who would harm us or put us down? None of these are matters of winning or losing. They are matters of acting correctly, matters of personal conduct.

I write this book during one of the saddest episodes of my

life – one I share now with some difficulty. The little girl we adopted in September is no longer with us. Just days before the final adoption order was granted, a new member of her birth-family came forward and petitioned for guardianship. Due to extraordinary circumstances in this particular case, that person hadn't been assessed before. Months of uncertainty followed while they were checked and in the end, given a positive assessment. The law favours birth family above adoption unless there's concern for safety and in this case there was none. After a brief and bruising legal battle, we realised we'd have to let her go.

The delicate issue of a hand-over came next. Our social workers felt we'd be unable to do this ourselves. There had been feelings of animosity during the court case. It was impossible to expect us to introduce the girl we considered our daughter to a family that would take her from us. They suggested handing her over to an interim foster-carer who would in turn introduce her to the birth family. This didn't sit well with me because she'd go through two traumatic changes instead of one. I asked Charmaigne if she felt she could meet the birth family. She didn't, but she supported me if I felt I could.

I did, and I told the social workers. I wanted to meet her new carer and, setting aside all differences, work together so our little girl wouldn't leave us for a complete stranger. The social workers doubted I could cope emotionally, but I assured them I could. How did I know? I just knew.

I've come to know what I'm capable of – not everything,

for sure – but I knew I could do this. I was determined, for the sake of our little girl, that she should have the gentlest changeover possible. To the credit of the birth family they agreed and I spent several bittersweet days introducing our little girl to her new family, and saying goodbye in the process.

People say they don't know how I did it. I simply saw the path I wanted to follow and I followed it. It was difficult and heart-breaking but it also gave me some unexpected happiness, to see where she was going and meet the people who'd be caring for her.

We asked our close family to come and say their goodbyes the day before the handover. The little girl was too young to understand what was going on and we didn't want a big outpouring of grief just before she left. On our final day together, a Sunday morning, I sat with Charmaigne and our other daughter Autumn and we said prayers and goodbyes. Charmaigne and Autumn left for church and I prepared to take my little girl for one last drive. Feeling the enormity of what I was about to do, I was worried I might crash. I took some deep breaths and for a moment I was back in my tent at summer camp, wrapping my gi around me and tying my belt. If I'd been a movie-star martial artist, I'd have broken open my weapons stash and headed into the Canadian wilderness where no one would ever find us. I'd have fought any number of line-ups to keep her, walked across fields of hot coals. But this was real life and there was no one to fight, only blame to cast around, and blame is a bitterness

I'd rather not taste. So I steadied my nerves and carried her to the car, fastened her seat belt and drove to the birth family's house. With the minimum of fuss and a final kiss I let her go and returned home.

Leading up to that day, there had been high emotions and plenty of tears. I expected them to return once I'd parked safely in the drive, but nothing came. I didn't feel cold or numb, simply calm and serene.

An hour later, I had a training session scheduled with Mike and Jake, our last before summer camp. Naturally, I'd considered cancelling it. The guys knew my situation so they understood. We'd agreed to wait and see how I felt. I texted them and asked them to come around – training was on. Having spent the best part of a year preparing together, I wanted our final session to be the most intense of all – thirty punishing rounds that would give them real confidence. I assured them it meant a lot to me to complete our final session, and it did. There are few things more rewarding than watching fighters you've coached revved up and raring to go. The guys came over and completed our toughest-ever session in good form. Then we knew our training was done.

That evening the calmness remained. My emotions were distant. The house was still and silent. We tidied away the cot and the baby stuff. It felt strange to put a coffee down on a low table without worrying about little hands reaching for it.

I kept expecting the emotions to flood in, but nothing came. I began to worry I'd shut myself down too hard. I was aware I needed to let go but all week I felt nothing but calm. I decided not to concern myself too much. Things have a habit of working themselves out.

I wondered about attending summer camp but it just felt right to be there, among friends, doing what I love, with good people all around me. I was looking forward to seeing Sensei Dan from Bristol, who I'm privileged to call a friend, and the men and women of DKK from around the country.

After two days of training, Sensei Gavin called an end to the fun and games of afternoon fitness and instructed all green belts and higher to report to the Field of Truth. I've described the results of Jake and Mike's tests. But some time after the mayhem of the fighting and the formalities of the presentations, the three of us found ourselves together, apart from the rest, in a quiet corner of the field. With tears in their eyes, these two big strong guys spoke of the nerves, the excitement, the relief and the humility that comes with going through this epic test. We'd come a long way together and our journey had ended in dramatic style. When they left to make the slow walk back to their tents, the emotion of the last week's events finally overtook me. Thoughts of the little girl I'd lost came back, not in a flood but in a gentle wave. I slipped from the Field of Truth to be alone for a while and walked back to my tent avoiding all contact.

The next day I was in charge of the grading for novices to green belt. I worked them hard in the mid-summer heat, on a rough field with no shade. Two ragged lines of boys and girls, men and women, students and professionals, mums and dads kicked and punched and sweated and fought their way to something that mattered to them. Two students who weren't grading joined in for extra training. I told them they were free to drop out any time they liked but after each water-break, they kept coming back. When I mentioned this to Sensei Gavin, he told them they were grading and they got new belts along with the rest.

I was impressed with all the determination on the field that day. I was equally impressed with the determination that, I knew, went on beforehand in the days leading up to summer camp. On the night before the grading and the long walk down to the field.

We all know how much easier it is to sit at home and watch the tennis with a glass of Pimm's. How much better we sleep on our own bed rather than an airbed that's deflated in the night. How carefree we feel on those warm summer weekends when we're not grading. It would have been tempting to listen to the whispers and make excuses but they wanted the belt, so they did the test and got the belt. So simple, and yet so hard. So important in so many ways.

This, then, is my karate, my 'Way' – and what it means to me. I hope that through sharing these thoughts and ideas, it will come to mean the same to you.

APPENDIX 1

Fighters' Insights

Some of the fighters who completed the test in recent years have been good enough to share their insights on training for the Thirty Man Kumite.

Reading their contributions has been enlightening, in particular those from the Bristol fighters who completed the test with no meddling on my part. Two things stand out for me, the first is the importance of finding a way to enjoy your training and keep yourself positive in the face of what can seem, for a lot of the time, like insurmountable odds. The second is that there's no one way or right way to do this, only your own way. Finding this 'way' is one of the most useful skills you'll ever develop in karate, and in everything else you do.

Siobhan Tierney, 2010

After a gratifying day of training during winter camp 2009 and a few cups of warm sake, I sneaked into my bunk bed reasonably confident that I'd agreed to attempt my Thirty Man nidan grading under DKK. But afterwards, this agreement ignited feelings of fear every time it entered my mind. This fear motivated me for the next eight months, and it took me towards standing in front of a long line of high-grade fighters from one of the UK's best karate clubs.

I started training with DKK London in 2002 and found it an immensely inspiring adventure. I left, regretfully, in 2004 when I moved to Birmingham but travelled down to train in the dojo as often as I could. I took my shodan in 2005 and had found the challenge of training so far away from DKK to be tough but rewarding. When I agreed to my nidan, I was living in Canterbury and realised that I faced the lonely challenge of 'remote training' again.

During those months of preparing for the nidan, I didn't really see the progress I was making, which was very disheartening. I was conditioning myself well, thanks to Kyokushin karate-ka in Margate and the helping strikes from the DKK karate-ka who knew the best way to help me was to hit me as often and as hard as they could. I was constantly increasing the speed of my runs and the intensity of my gym sessions, so it always felt like a slog. Physically I felt drained and far from fit. I spent so many hours either training, getting to training or thinking about training that I never felt rested. Even when my body was allowed to stop, my mind was still clamped firmly onto the grading. I was obsessed and it was powerful and exhausting to be allowed to be so bloody-minded.

One of the fundamental aspects of my training was my one-to-one Sunday sessions with Goran, who had not only completed his own nidan, but had also helped others in the preparation for theirs. Here, my training was specifically geared towards that 34-minute test and the strategies I would employ to get through it. I was able to see how my footwork and power were developing. I had the chance to talk with someone who was so eloquently able to explain how he and other karate-ka had got through the training and grading. Goran helped me develop my natural strengths whilst also helping me to notice the areas I was lagging in and how to improve them. It wasn't until I was in the thick of the grading that I realised how important the strategy we developed actually was.

During summer camp 2010 there were moments when Sensei Gavin reminded the DKK members that the Thirty Man line up is a soul-baring grading where each participant is stripped bare, one minute at a time by their peers, until it is seen if they are still standing or not. The terrifying truth that I was about to put myself through this was inescapable and I felt petrified. But I got through it.

Embarking on the nidan offered me opportunities to find things out about myself that few people have the chance to discover. To be allowed to attempt this test was a privilege. I had seen the souls of others stripped bare on that field before. I knew what I was getting myself into. But to actually go through that process was immense and it has equipped me to deal with these challenges that life continually presents. Now, for me, it's not about preparing for a nidan, it's about living up to it.

Simon Mackown, 2011

My first ever session was at DKK summer school. While a truly inspiring event in itself, the defining moment for me was witnessing Mark Salomone and Genevieve Charles complete the Thirty Man Kumite and earn their nidan grade. What struck me most was not the physicality, or the level of fitness required, but the mental strength that they both showed in completing the task. It was the idea of exploring how far I could push myself mentally as well as physically that ultimately made me join DKK.

Training to be ready for nidan is, in many ways, tougher than the grading itself. The early morning starts, the daily training and the sacrifices meant that at times it felt relentless, unrewarding and lonely. To be frank, there were times when I simply hated karate. However, it's vital that you get your head in the right space if training is going to be effective.

This is where the years of training and discipline help. I also found it useful to draft a training plan for each week which I stuck to religiously, whether I wanted to or not. It kept me honest with myself about the preparation I had done.

I rehearsed the grading over and over in my head many times before, in particular the fights with people who I knew who would really push me to my limits. I planned how I was going to fight these people and while these plans didn't always work out, it at least prevented me from worrying about the fights beforehand. The key to getting your head in the right place for grading is preparation. I was able to draw confidence from the fact that I had trained hard, was the fittest I had been and that my fighting had improved significantly. I honestly knew before I stepped onto the field that there was no more I could have done, there was nothing I could do now to change things, it was going to be hard, it was going to hurt, I was going to be tired.

Because I was resigned to my fate, I was unburdened by fear, worry and doubt, and this freed me up to enjoy the task ahead. Moreover, because I was more relaxed, I was able to fight and move freely. However, simply accepting your fate is not enough on its own, you have to have self-belief to succeed. I had decided long before the event that I was a nidan. I wasn't taking the grading to prove myself but to stop the thirty men in front of me from taking away what was rightfully mine. This wasn't something I vocalised, I didn't strut about boasting about my prowess, but approaching the grading in this manner helped to give me confidence to succeed.

Doing the Thirty Man Kumite is a once-in-a-lifetime experience which I was able to savour and even enjoy, but only because I had prepared properly in advance, physically and mentally.

Katharine Winstanley, 2012

I'd never expected to attempt my nidan grading, but when I achieved shodan in 2009, I knew I'd have to at least try. There was no reason not to – other than fear – and that didn't seem good enough. However, training for my shodan had taken a significant toll on my general well-being, so I was determined to find a way that worked better for me. I knew I'd have at least three years before the grading so I considered the main objective of the next year to relax, recover and regain my enjoyment of karate. I didn't reduce the number of sessions I attended, but I did reduce the amount of additional fitness I did, and also took the opportunity to try some new things, like ballet. In the second year, I aimed to increase my basic fitness, focusing on specific areas of weakness. I also completed my first marathon, knowing marathon training would be incompatible with the more specific nidan training I'd start in the following year.

When it came to the third year, I took the time to consider what it was I really needed to train, and how to achieve my aim of training hard while staying relaxed. The time away from the constant pressures of gradings had also given me time to consider why some of my gradings had gone so much better than others.

While my karate and fitness had steadily improved, the same was not true of my grading performance. I considered the ones I felt happy with, and identified what was different about them. I'd felt confident and determined going in, and done my best to stay positive throughout. As a result, I'd enjoyed the gradings. In contrast, those that had gone less well, I'd entered with a sense of defeat. While the Thirty Man seems on the face of it a primarily physical challenge, I felt this wasn't going to be the most important aspect for me. Like all gradings, it's a test of mind, body and spirit, and I needed to work on all three.

The learning aspect of my nidan training was about unpicking my sparring and trying to take a more considered approach. This wasn't about adding any particular new techniques, but more about how to use combinations, distancing, and tailoring my approach to different partners. None of it was new, but it involved thinking about what I was doing rather than just reacting. I also spent a lot of time working on kata, more so than for any previous grading, but with a focus on application – not in the sense of practicing set bunkai, but more in terms of considering more carefully where my opponent was and what I was doing about it.

In my physical training, I trained at the karate club three times a week. I reduced the number and length of runs each week, focusing on hills and speed work. I also had access to a work gym with a bag, and I would do thirty rounds of pad drills, focusing on the aspects I wanted to bring into my sparring. I took a circuits class and did other plyometric training, and I took up Bikram yoga for active recovery. I was already training frequently before I entered this phase, so the change was in focus, working more on intense efforts and quick recovery. In class I did more hard sparring and 'The Wall' – standing against a wall while everyone takes it in turn to hit you for one minute. I did each a maximum of once a week to allow for repair and recovery.

The biggest challenge was conquering my fear of the test. Initially my main tactic was just to ensure I enjoyed this stage of my training, and to balance training with relaxation. At the time I had a long commute to work. So I arranged with my manager to use accrued leave and work four days a week in the months leading up to the grading. I planned plenty of things that didn't relate to training: a concert, a trip to the theatre, a holiday for afterwards.

I also used the opportunity to try new things. I began swimming at an open air pool and even took some trapeze classes. As the grading drew closer, I remained calm. The nature of the grading helped because I knew exactly what I'd have to do, so I focused on training specifically for that. I was confident that my training was giving me the best possible chance, and while there might be more that I could do, I didn't think there was more that I should do.

The day of the grading came. In contrast to the day of my shodan grading, I didn't feel sick. I felt calm. I trained during the day, then went back to my tent and had a cup of tea. I got dressed and walked down to the field. Other people seemed more nervous for me than I was. I knew it would be extremely difficult, but I knew I could do it.

During the grading, I was expecting everyone to hit hard, but I was still surprised at how hard they all fought, especially some of the smaller and lower grades. I was also surprised at how little I felt the pain. It was almost as if I'd stepped outside my body. Some fights went well, others less so. I focused on the fight at hand, without worrying about what had been or what was to come. Unexpectedly, a mantra came to me, one that my yoga teacher had constantly repeated, and it got me through the worst fights. She would say, 'concentrate, meditate', and tell us to stop worrying about the poses we'd done, and those that were to come, and just focus on what we were doing right then. This helped me to take each fight as it came, not worrying about those that hadn't gone so well, and not worrying about who I'd be facing next, or the growing thunderstorm!

As soon as I finished my last fight, my body went into shock and I struggled to breath. Once I'd regained my composure, I remember people crowding around to congratulate me. Sempai Goran made a point of saying it was the strongest performance he'd ever seen from me, and in the toughest test. This was good to hear because it meant my hard training, and above all my mental preparation, had worked.

The Thirty Man Kumite is the biggest challenge I've ever undertaken. I'm thankful to have had the opportunity to test myself in this way, and pleased that I ignored my first instinct that it wasn't for me.

Ragi McFadden, 2013

At my first ever summer camp in 2001 I saw the first female attempt the Thirty Man Kumite in DKK, Charlie Mulholland, and I remember being in absolute awe and wonder at her achievement. I thought to myself: that is what I want to do one day, but it was a long way to go. Twelve years later, I began my training towards the Thirty Man Kumite.

I was very nervous and doubted my ability to succeed. People gave me a lot of advice on how to go about my training in the lead up because they cared but I found it all rather confusing and contradictory. It was not until I started my training with Goran that I felt I was making progress. This was because he was able to identify specific areas in my training that required improvement and encourage me to build on my strengths. Visualisation of my line up helped me to feel mentally prepared.

Many of my close friends from the dojo showed a lot of support and encouragement which helped motivate me and keep me going during tough times.

The advice I would give to people is to relax your mind and body, especially when training, so you are able to fully benefit from the training and make progress. Being anxious and nervous results in you tensing your muscles which inhibits flow and ease of movement.

The after-feeling of completing the nidan test for me was euphoric, a total sense of achievement and I hold it close to my heart when facing difficult times.

Simon Clinch, 2013

When I first witnessed a Thirty Man Kumite (I was grading for Shodan-Ho at the time) I remember clearly thinking: 'I could never do that' and 'I don't ever want to do that'.

A couple of years later, my mindset had changed from fear to an outright desire to face the challenge. Ironically, at the same time my sensei, Gavin Mulholland, offered me the opportunity to face the test. The timing was clearly right.

Those in my dojo who had gone before me gave me some good advice and ideas about how to train for this most physically challenging of gradings. A common theme was to have a fairly rigid training regime, six days a week with one day of rest, focus on strength training, technique and conditioning in the first six months and concentrate on escalating cardiovascular training in the final months. Leave the final week to rest and recover. Clearly regular dojo training was a big feature to build on techniques and conditioning. Another aspect was running or sprinting, particularly in the months approaching the grading.

I had to take this advice and apply it differently, as my circumstances with family and work meant my location during the weeks would be unpredictable (London or Henley with no regular pattern) and I would be also be training on my own, since I live over 90 minutes from the dojo. Furthermore, running was not viable due to persistent back and knee injuries. So I had to look at what

I had available to me: the London dojo once a week, a gym at my work headquarters, with 2 punch bags, some work colleagues interested in sparring, but from different martial arts backgrounds (boxing and Krav Maga) and a skipping rope, punch-bag and weights at home.

My training started with the mind. I gave up alcohol. I also made myself visualise being attacked by the toughest fighters in the dojo all the time – while walking down the street, while playing with my children, while sitting at my desk at work. I found this an invaluable psychological tool to help me remain motivated.

Initially, the physical aspects of training began with as much dojo training as I could fit in, seeking out the best fighters in the club whenever there was sparring. When not in London, I would visit the gym at work to focus on weights, building up my quad strength, chest, arms and abs. Later in the day I would go back to the gym to work on the punch-bag. The punch-bag was a core part of my regime, and probably the most helpful tool outside the dojo. It was a good conditioning aid and a replacement for running. I also used a cross-trainer for cardio fitness.

There were two core training programmes I used on the punch-bag and cross-trainer. I mimicked a line-up and set 1 minutes intervals of flat-out effort aimed at getting to my peak heart rate, interspersed by 10 second breaks over 20 rounds. This takes around 25 minutes and served as a warm-up or finale to my work-out. The second option was to use tabata: 8 rounds of 20 seconds at flat-out pace, with 10 second breaks in between, for a set of 5 minutes.

I'd do this 3 times for a 15 minute set, again pushing my heart rate to its peak. Both exercises were important for training short rapid bursts and quick recoveries, important traits for surviving a Thirty Man Kumite.

I also found some work colleagues interested in sparring. This was useful at first, but my strength soon leapt far beyond their capabilities and it just became too easy, if not a little dangerous (I broke a sparring partner's ribs).

How did my training pay off? Well I completed the challenge, and I was pleased with my fitness. However, I was not entirely pleased by my performance. For one thing, while I focused on training, I had failed to think enough about strategy. I planned simply to put everything I had into every fight, and that was unsustainable. Furthermore, while I was the fittest and strongest I had ever been, I suspect my conditioning could have been better. This is the problem with training in isolation. I would urge any candidate training remotely to find another hard martial arts club, if only to have a consistent flow of high-impact sparring in their training regime. Am I being hard on myself? Maybe, but that's my character as a martial artist – a constant pursuit of mastery and perfection, inevitably littered with failures and disappointments along the way!

It's worth mentioning too the emotional impact of the Thirty Man Kumite. After training hard and single-mindedly for a year, the immediate aftermath of the challenge was met with a huge emotional dump. I was unable to hold back tears, not helped by my body's uncontrollable shaking in a state of shock. And because of my somewhat negative assessment of my performance, I tried to maintain a high level of training in the months that followed – a bad idea as my body desperately needed a break (I was seeing a chiropractor every two weeks in the final four months of training).

The one thing I am confident of is the training and experience has made me a much better martial artist, and not just in sparring – kata, technique, and mindset as well. I am truly thankful for the experience.

Andy Bremerkamp, 2013

I had been in the line-up of the Thirty Man test for others a number of times in the years before requesting mine. Each one I'd seen, or been part of, made me want to do it myself, eventually, more and more. Some of the tests I'd seen essentially involved the participant standing and taking a beating and just continuously getting up off the floor to be beaten down again. Fair play – they kept getting up.

A few tests, though, stood out in that the participant looked reasonably in control throughout and continued fighting with skill and energy to the last man. This is how I wanted to try and do mine, not just get through it and taking a beating, but hopefully staying strong and still giving it back at the end. One of the key things I picked up from talking to the guys that stood out previously was the importance of fitness. They were good fighters too, but had very good fitness and cardio strength.

Simon Mackown gave me a simple approach, which I think he used: if you could run on your limit as fast as you could for forty minutes, then this would give you a basic grounding of cardio needed for the time to do the Thirty Man.

This formed the base of my additional training in that I would try and run at least once a week for forty minutes as hard and fast as I could. I then added steep, short hill runs to the end of each longer run and incrementally increased the number of times I hit the hill in the weeks before the test.

The dojo training continued as usual, but with the added help and individual focus on me from Sensei Dan and the other guys who'd been through it. There was a lot of emphasis on movement and keeping out of range, making them move to you and obviously the general beatings and gradual build-up of ten, fifteen and twenty man line-ups. These are definitely key in order to build the confidence that you can get through a certain number of fights.

Mentally, I tried to look at it as just something to get done and to not let it seem bigger than any other grading or challenge, and therefore overwhelming. I didn't stop drinking a few beers at the weekend for example, as this would make it seem like it was somehow a harder challenge than any other and I would be putting it on a pedestal and adding pressure. Obviously the truth was that it was much, much more of a challenge than anything I had done. The actual event was so much harder than I thought it would be. Even though I knew everyone would be attacking hard during their one minute of fighting, the sheer intensity of each fighter was very difficult to try and control, both physically and mentally. In the line-ups in the dojo I had generally felt in control, but in the actual event, especially the first ten fights, it was a struggle to not be overwhelmed.

Even with what I thought was very good fitness, in the short breaks between fights I was gasping for air. Most of it is a blur but the few bits that I remember are: throwing someone near the beginning, axe-kicking Smiley (I never used that kick before!) and being kicked backwards by Big Dave's front-kick, but thinking this is okay as a breather because he's miles away! And really getting into and enjoying the last few fights, knowing I was near the end. As with all gradings, at the end I felt that I should have done it much better, although I felt like I had half achieved my goal of not just being a punching bag getting up off the floor all the time.

It also surprised me how emotional I was at the end. I actually broke down with tears a bit, although not as much as Simon Clinch!

On reflection, I think cardio fitness is definitely a big factor. If you can keep moving, you can limit the damage by not just standing like a target in one spot. I think mentally, you have to accept that you're going to get a beating, no matter how good you are technically, and not back off or shy away from any strikes as they will hurt and damage more. Easier said than done!

Ben Hung, 2013

After a few years as shodan, I knew that in order to push myself to the next level as a martial artist I eventually had to take the most revered grading test in the DKK syllabus. It was a great test to put myself forward for in so many ways: first, to seek the approval of my sensei, which was daunting in itself. Then the dawning reality, after approval, that you may have just offered yourself as a punch-bag to thirty of the best fighters in the association. Questioning your own ability comes into play and asking yourself if you're worthy to be in the same league as those who succeeded before you. What if I'm not fit enough on the day? What if I take a bone-crushing dead leg early on and have to hobble my way through the grading? What if I get winded or knocked out? How am I going to fight *insert name*? etc.

The grading itself has always been a spectacular and emotional event in DKK and you can't help feeling inspired, regardless of what grade you are or if you even train at all. So for the one good shot I had at this I didn't want to be remembered as someone who scraped through. I wanted to be a different, more evolved fighter from the moment I requested the attempt to the moment I finished the last fight. For me that was the point of the test and the training. If I was prepared to go into this, making sacrifices and involving other people, I wanted something to show for it all.

Initially, my training consisted of establishing a good base fitness and strength which would eventually peak to high intensity workouts and plyometrics in the final months. This included bag work, jump-rope, pad work and sparring. At my peak, I was training two times a day, six days a week, religiously adhering to a tailored timetable. I wanted to emulate the hard sparring and intensity of the grading as much as possible, so a lot of what I regarded as superfluous training was out and everything I trained for had to have a reason and purpose.

But that was the fitness part and I didn't want my training to consist of just a 'get fit' regime.

A huge, and integral, part of my schedule was seeing Goran for additional training. I needed good technique and strategy and after seeing what a tremendous job he did, years before, with Dominic Du Plooy – a skilful karate-ka but the smallest male black belt at the time – I wanted a part of that too. With the right training and mindset, they pioneered a style and conditioning that made completing the nidan grading actually feasible to the more 'normal' fighters in the club.

I wasn't exactly sure what Goran had planned for me. I was aware that he tailored candidates' training individually to their size and skills and worked on their weaknesses whilst emphasising their strengths. It would be intriguing to see what he had in store for me. Actually,

I was expecting some sort of military style boot-camp but to my surprise Goran's training session consisted of fundamental footwork drills, pad work and specially tailored kihon drills that emphasised counter-fighting and attacks while maintaining form and technique.

Initially, I was quite stiff and awkward with these sequences but after the months of constant drilling and determination these evolved into something very different. No longer was I robotic in my movements but I was more graceful, efficient and fluid. I understood then that Goran had taken my karate back to basics and tidied me up in the process. In doing so he vastly improved my timing, precision, speed and coordination – essential tools in the striking game.

By the time the grading came, I knew I was ready and had trained as hard I could have done. It was hard, as I had expected, but by then I knew the grading was the final piece of the puzzle for me to fill in after a long journey.

I did what I had set out to when I first requested to attempt the grading. That is, with the help of many people, I feel I have improved in so many ways as a martial artist and I had the privilege of being allowed to go back and tidy up the holes in my game and become a better fighter in the process. For me, the nidan belt has indeed been an enlightening experience where I've been allowed to perfect many aspects of my karate.

Daniel Bard, 2014

At first my feeling was definitely fear of what could happen in the grading – serious injury or failure – but also fear of the training that, I knew, would consume most of my free time for a long period. It wasn't ideal at the time and probably never is for those stepping forward.

The biggest difference in training, without a doubt, was the mental side, especially having to visualise the line-up every Sunday and the fighters I'd be facing. This meant I was completely comfortable at the start of the grading. I had spent time beforehand looking at each of the thirty people in the line and felt no fear of what was to come. In fact the opposite happened and I became excited and energised by the prospect. In hindsight it probably enabled me to conserve enough energy to get through.

My advice for those facing the test would be that you should warn people, especially close family, to support you as much as possible and not make too many demands on your time. Also, speak to everyone who has completed the test and get their perspective on the training they did and what you should be doing.

Train with someone else who is also going for the test. This is especially helpful if they are fitter than you and more dedicated, as it will inspire you to train harder. Train as much as possible but don't overdo it or injure yourself. After class, do at least 10 rounds of one minute, ideally sparring, but if you're injured then sparring type exercises: pad-work, skipping or shadow-boxing.

Acknowledge that what you've signed up for is an element of reality – it's not called the Field of Truth by chance so be prepared for what that truth could be.

Juha Makinen, 2014

When I first saw a Thirty Man Kumite I thought I'd never ever do it. It was quite something to witness and I hadn't expected to see anything like it.

Danny Bard tried to persuade me to do it with him in 2013 but I didn't warm to the idea. He kept trying to get me on board, he was very persistent – you know how much he likes to talk! Then I spent I bit of time with Ben Hung when he trained for his Thirty Man. When I saw he managed it in such a solid way – not getting injured and even looking effortless all way the through (although that's probably the wrong word) it made me think, 'Bloody hell, there is a way to get through the line-up and stay alive'. I think that encouraged me.

Since I was already forty-five years old, I knew that postponing it any further would only make the whole idea shaky. The next day I told Sensei Gavin I'd like to do the Thirty Man. It was at the evening barbecue on the last day of summer camp and he asked me how many beers I'd drunk. He even repeated the question two more times, but once he realised I wasn't drunk and I was keen to give it my best shot, he accepted.

After a brutal Five Man 'taster' in January, I remember a chat with Goran when we walked to the park near his place. He asked me what my game plan was going to be. The Five Man 'beat up' was a real eye-opener. It highlighted how, even if I prepared hard, there was no way of keeping such a high intensity through thirty fights. I had a moment when I was a bit concerned as I didn't have any game plan as such. However, the idea crystalised after thinking back over the Thirty Man fights I'd seen before. Guys like Oisin Carr, Dragos Voiculescu, Ben Hung, Simon Mackown, Andy Bremerkamp, Michael Christian and female fighters like Ragi McFadden and Siobhan Tierney had all managed to keep their fights in 'compact form'. They seemed to have a plan and were able to stick to it all the way through, rarely getting sucked into energy-consuming grappling, keeping it simple but fighting hard at the same time. The balance just seemed to work. This eventually helped in devising my game plan. The recovery time between fights was going to be very short so I needed to avoid getting involved in close-in fighting. It would sap my energy and escalate the risk of ending up a punch bag. It would also make me an easy target for vicious low kicks and heavy punches. So the game plan was to keep myself mobile and use the field to move around and stop the low kicks from getting through for as long as possible. Avoid unnecessary body tension, especially tightness in the shoulders, thus saving energy. Take the fights as they come and don't bother too much about what's coming next. Keep it all simple because once you get tired, all fancy ideas and strategies go straight out of the window. Attack using fast high kicks whenever possible. This helps to give you distance based on a simple rule that nobody likes getting kicked in the head.

Regarding the mental decision not to go down, I don't know how to explain this. My objective was to fight on unless an injury stopped me. There was this 'mental element' knowing that facing certain fighters was going to hurt. In the end I did go down a few times – probably three times in the last four fights – but none was caused solely by the pain but more from the force of the kicks and being so tired. I don't think I can explain the mental decision logically. It was simply knowing that if everything held together it was going to be easier and less painful to keep going on.

One very important motto I remember when we trained was not to show that I'm tired or injured during the fights, including in the breaks between the fights. Showing weakness is like throwing gasoline into the fire or showing a red flag to a raging bull. It will just escalate the intensity of the punches and kicks. The guys in the line-up know they can attack hard without worrying about getting hurt. Once you drop this 'mental guard' the real problems start. I saw excellent, very strong fighters taking a terrible beat up in the last few fights and it made me realise you need to be 'better than well prepared'.

Rob Curtis, 2014

I originally aimed at completing my nidan in 2012, but tore my ACL knee ligament in training in late 2011. Clearly this was a blow, but it gave me a goal to aim at throughout the subsequent rehab.

As well as making sure I was training as much as I could in the dojo, I also added CrossFit for strength and interval training and Muay Thai sessions for drills and conditioning. Regular physio treatments were useful as well to help me get through the increased training load without further injury. I was training around six times a week, and kept a spreadsheet to track what I was doing, and ensure I was resting as well!

It became clear, though, that despite the rehab and the training I was doing, my leg wasn't going to cope with the abnormal load it would take during the kumite. Following advice from my physio and discussion with Sensei Dan, I was able to wear a knee brace for the event.

This leads to one of the three most important things for me in the preparation period: make things familiar. I wore the knee brace all the time in training to get used to it. I wore the same gloves and gum-shield. I went running and did CrossFit in the shoes I was going to wear.

The second key element was to use my imagination all the time while training. If I was running then every minute would be another round of the kumite. I tried to develop an approach where I was always transposing my training to the kumite, and repeating the mantra, 'it's only

GORAN POWELL

a minute, you can push through it,' every time things were hard.

The final point was that I wanted to enter the field happy that I had prepared as well as I could. That meant I knew I'd followed my training plan, not cut corners, and not done things 'half assed'.

I completed my nidan in 2014. When I came to fight, last in my group, I was stunned by how fast people came out the gate for the first few rounds, even though I'd fought on the other side of the kumite many times. I don't remember much about it, just a few key moments. I remember enjoying it at the time, but also working on auto-pilot for a lot of it. I was happy with some things, for example working lots of throws and clinches into my fights. But devastated to have been knocked out in round 24. It took me a few seconds to get back to my feet and be able to fight again, but my performance afterwards wasn't one I was happy with at all.

With a few years' distance though, getting up and carrying on after being knocked out is the thing that made it for me. I could have stopped, but didn't.

I was so happy to have completed the challenge although very down for some months afterwards. I had achieved the thing I had been working on for years. But that meant the goal had gone. I was battered and bruised, and although wearing a black gi, it took me some time to get over an element of 'imposter syndrome' about it. I think being able to help train the next set of people coming though, and developing goals both in and out of karate, has helped with that. Maybe it just takes a couple of years of perspective.

My interest in training methods outside the dojo has really been piqued, and so now I am studying to be a personal trainer to inform my own training, and to help others with theirs.

Darren Heywood, 2014

My introduction to the Thirty Man was at summer school about ten years ago. Here I watched a fellow karate-ka step up and face thirty full contact fights. It was truly a remarkable show of courage, determination and spirit. Over the next few years that I watched and participated in the Thirty Man Kumite, I'd walk away each time thinking I'd never be good enough to face such a challenge. Then one year something changed and I started to think maybe I could do it, maybe I could face such a test. It was then that I decided to put myself forward and began training for my own line-up.

First question was, how do I go about preparing? I had an idea for the physical side, but what about the mental side? I knew I had to face a few demons. One of my biggest obstacles was I thought I was not a good fighter and everybody else was so much better than me. Also I felt I had age against me (I wasn't recovering from the knocks like before) and I had a medical condition, a mild heart arrhythmia that had never stopped me from training hard, but it was one more thing that played on my mind.

I spoke to the others who'd faced the Thirty Man and this was invaluable. It helped me put together a tried and tested programme that fitted my lifestyle. I planned my week into training slots with two sessions per day, morning and evening. These could be a karate class or a lighter session if I'd trained hard in the morning. I made sure I had at least one rest day a week, and maybe two if my body needed it. That is one thing I learned, probably the hard way: to listen to my body. If I needed an extra rest day I took it, and always came back stronger.

My programme was set out over ten months. Each session I made sure I wore my mouth-guard so I got conditioned to it. In my garage, I wore my gi for the same reason. Another thing that incentivised me was the photo of the Thirty Man line-up on the wall, which I'd look at each time I trained.

For the first five months I concentrated on endurance training: running, cross-training, swimming or bag-work. On the bag, I'd focus on combinations and footwork, which was important for me because I'm one of the smaller guys in the club. I had to learn to move! I also fitted in weight training twice a week and a weekly Bootcamp session.

Over the next five months my endurance work tapered off to be replaced with high intensity training: tabata, hill sprints and sparring. I'd arrive early at Sunday Bootcamp to spar with a friend. Any opportunity I had to spar, I would spar. This allowed me to try new things. However, through the advice of others and trial and error, I deliberately kept to simple combinations.

I also tried to keep relaxed, as I soon learnt being tight and full-on drained my energy fast and destroyed my breathing. I tried smiling while sparring as this made the experience a little more enjoyable and put me into a positive frame of mind. On the days I had karate, I would try and get there early and find anybody to spar with. I fought all grades so I could work on different aspects. With the less experienced guys I'd imagine they were the biggest, toughest fighters in the club and focus on my footwork and my guard, trying not to get hit. In class, we'd have a conditioning session that's referred to affectionately as 'The Wall'. Essentially, I had to stand against the wall while an opponent would condition me with punches and kicks.

Then came summer school and a myriad of emotions, everything from complete fear to overwhelming positivity. The sessions have slipped from memory because my mind was elsewhere. I just wanted to get onto the Field of Truth and get started. Unfortunately, this was not to happen as my arrhythmia decided to make an unannounced appearance. I'm not sure why it did, it just did. Perhaps it was the lack of sleep, the extreme of emotions I was feeling, the anxiety, all came together in the perfect storm. My mind was all over the place. The mental strength I had was gone. Doubts and negative thoughts flooded my mind and these were compounded by the situation I was in. How on earth could I face the

Thirty Man in this condition? I spoke with both senseis and told them my unfortunate news. I can't remember exactly what was said, but during the conversation they showed great compassion, concern and support. Quite rightly, they left the decision to me. I knew I was fit enough, but I felt mentally and physically drained. As well as dealing with my own health, I was also thinking about my family and how it would affect them if anything went wrong. I had to make a decision. I chose not to grade. To say this was heart-wrenching is an understatement. I felt physically gutted. I felt such a failure. I felt I had let myself and others down. All that training, time and effort, wasted. I now had to break the news to my fellow nidan candidates. I kept it short and to the point. I wished them luck and walked away. I didn't want my negativity to rub off on them.

Once summer school was over and normality returned I knew I'd made the right decision, but still it was a hard pill to swallow. I took the next month very easy until, after seeing various doctors, I was given the all clear to start training again.

The condition I have is very common and a number of well know athletes suffer from it. After discussions with sensei, it was agreed that I was to re-attempt the Thirty Man at winter school. I'd already spoken with my family at great lengths and we all agreed I could attempt it once more. But if I had the slightest flutter, either during my training or during the Thirty Man, I was to pull out. I agreed, for obvious reasons.

Over the next couple of months I continued my training as before, but subconsciously I knew I had to be a lot more self-aware of how I felt. It's hard enough facing the Thirty Man when you're fit and uninjured. Going into it with an injury, however small, can be psychologically damaging. I knew that if I was to complete the Thirty Man I had to be mentally prepared.

My training went by without any glitches and it was soon time to head off to winter school. This time I felt different. I had a different mindset. I felt more relaxed, and more in control.

My grading was sprung on me. I'd been told I was to grade on Saturday, but when I arrived on Friday night I was told I was grading in two hours! I felt good – no nerves, very positive. In my head I was going to treat this like a sparring session on a Wednesday night. This helped me stay calm and in control. An hour before the grading I felt restless and agitated, so a friend and I went for a walk around the camp as a distraction. We went through Tensho kata in the middle of a field as dusk was falling, which was really surreal, but it did the trick.

The Thirty Man was a blur. I can remember a few fights here and there. At first my game plan seemed to be working. I wanted to stay light on my feet, move a lot and block/counter. All was going well and I felt great, mentally and physically relaxed and in control. But this was short lived. I'm not sure when, but I remember suddenly feeling shattered. My game plan had gone out the window. I was just trying to survive. I'd lost the ability to think, to react, and my legs and arms felt like lead weights, unable to respond to the commands I was trying to give them. I got through twenty fights and had a short break. At this point I wanted to quit, walk away, but something inside kept saying 'just one more fight'. I'm not sure why but I had to walk along the line and look the last ten fighters in the eye. Maybe this was a mental thing as I'd faced these fighters every time I'd trained in my garage. I remember coming face to face with Sempai Goran and telling him I wanted a hard fight. He replied with a big 'Osu'. The last ten fights were not pretty, but I eventually faced Goran, who gave me exactly what I'd asked for. Then it was finished and I was done. I'd faced the Thirty Man and survived, in every sense of the word!

The rest of winter school went by and I trained as much as my body allowed. I was battered and bruised, but didn't care. I was now a nidan. Interestingly, the elation was short-lived. Once I'd returned to family life, I felt something of a fraud. Did I deserve to be a nidan? I felt my performance could have been better. There were things I'd wanted to do during the fights, but couldn't. I felt others had done a better job than me. I felt lost, with no direction. If I was feeling like this, should I really have put myself, my health and my family in jeopardy?

Those demons were hard to get past. What helped was finding a new focus. During my training I'd enjoyed using kettlebells, so I set myself a goal to get better with them. I also needed to focus on something new in karate, so I chose kata to improve my understanding. Talking to the other nidans helped me to realise they too had had the same doubts, and the decisions I'd made along the way were the right ones. As time passed, I felt I'd returned to my old self and wearing the black gi felt right, like I'd earned it and deserved it. Now I've finally put those demons to rest. The doubts I had in my fighting abilities have gone and I feel confident. I know there's still so much I can learn, but that's the great thing about karate, there's always room for improvement, whatever your grade.

Going through all the training, overcoming demons and setbacks and facing the Thirty Man line-up has also allowed me to face other stressful situations outside the dojo head on. If I can face the Thirty Man and get through, I really can face anything.

Philippa Lovegrove, 2015

For me the nidan grading was my chance to prove myself within the club as a martial artist. I wasn't particularly happy with my shodan-ho or shodan gradings. I passed, so I must have done what was required or there's no way Senseis Lewis and Mulholland would have graded me, but I was focused on the areas I felt went badly and was dissatisfied. I believed this was my chance to do well and show everyone what I could achieve.

As soon as I had spoken with Sensei Lewis (the first lesson back after Summer School 2014) about going for nidan, I started a diary of my training. I think the diary allowed me to follow my progress and keep my training on track. I could easily see the weeks when, due to illness or commitments, training was lacking, and this allowed me to step it up in the following weeks. I didn't want to go down the route of having a very rigid training plan on a spreadsheet with months of training mapped out ahead of me. It felt unrealistic and potentially de-motivating to plan like that. I had a more fluid approach with three phases. Before Christmas, Phase One, work on my base level of fitness. I'd read about improving your aerobic fitness, and that by increasing the amount you can do aerobically it would improve endurance. So I started doing long, slow runs using a heart-rate monitor to make sure I was training with a low bpm. After Christmas Phase Two was just increasing the intensity. I ditched the long runs and did more strength training. Karate lessons allowed time for working on sparring technique. Phase Three was the final push, blasting it, before winding down the last couple of weeks before the grading.

A large part of my training independently involved running. One of my favourite runs, and the most challenging, was a trail type route that included steep inclines, rocky and uneven grassy surfaces, winding though woodland, steps, and some hill-sprints at the end. It was a route I ran a lot anyway but, unintentionally, it proved to be a big benefit for the grading. The Field of Truth is quite uneven and on a slight incline. Being used to moving about on a very uneven surface I'm sure helped my footwork and strengthened my legs and ankles for stability.

The running on such a familiar route also gave me time to think and focus on the task ahead. The mental battle to get where you need to be for Summer School and the grading is full of ups and downs. When I was running, I would visualise the fights and give myself a talking to about what I needed to put it to get results. Running up the steep incline, I'd imagine Sensei Lewis and Sensei Mulholland sat on a log at the top, looking down with distain at my seemingly feeble efforts to run as fast as I could to the top without stopping.

Early on in my training the tragic death of a fellow karate-ka, and the battle against cancer by another, brought everything into focus for me. The passing of John Sowesby really affected me. He wasn't a close friend, but being of a similar age and with a son of similar age makes you think about how precious life is, and how you can't afford to waste any opportunity. It made me more determined to give it my all. And knowing with what inner strength and positivity my friend was facing cancer was an inspiration. One thing I've drawn from this, or at least now truly appreciate from the experience of training and achieving nidan, is that when faced with a seemingly impossible or enormous task, or situation, you have to approach it positively. You will never get to where you need to be with one step, but if you keep making positive moves with the focus on the end goal, you will achieve it. This realisation and approach has already been tried and tested in my personal life and I'm in no doubt that I'm a better person for having gone through the nidan grading. It is so much more than a physical challenge.

The training process was a rollercoaster of emotions. There were lessons when, after sparring, I was close to tears, believing there was no way I could ever get through the thirty fights, and others when I felt almost invincible. For a while I was particularly stressed and caught up on the idea that I wasn't sparring enough with the high grade girls, and so wasn't properly preparing for what I'd be facing. For the most part I was sparring with nidans Rob and Darren and the other high grade men at the Portishead club. As time went on, I came to the conclusion that this was actually an advantage, both physically and mentally. My training involved sparring against men who were usually taller and considerably heavier than me, and the grading would consist of women who were generally the same height and similar build.

My advice to anyone undertaking this or similar would be: keep a training diary or record to track your progress. I wrote in every piece of advice I was given after sparring, how I felt after training. It helped to keep things in focus.

Listen to your body. If you are exhausted from training don't try and train through it, take a rest day, take two rest days, you'll train better for it.

Keep a positive mindset. Keep taking positive steps towards the goal. In sparring, even if you are defending, do it with the feeling that you are moving forward not that you are being beaten back. Be open to advice and learn from others who have done it before, or who are good fighters.

You have to give it everything you have. I had to battle with myself to give it my all, it's easy to hold back and have the excuse that if I'd trained harder I would have done better. I wanted to do a good job, I didn't want to struggle though. The weekend of Summer School I felt no nerves. Grading and competitions always made me really nervous. I was concerned that when it came to the weekend and directly before the grading I would be so nervous I would go blank or waste much needed energy. But surprisingly, to myself and others I'm sure, I felt perfectly calm. I knew what was coming and I was ready for it. Just before, I began to feel quite emotional, not from nerves, more that the moment had arrived after all the build up. A friend helped me calm myself and focus again. I went down to the Field of Truth, I stood in the corner with my eyes shut and my training 'theme tune', Foo Fighters, 'One by One' in my head. That's all I had to do get through, one by one. I felt I did well. I was elated after, I still haven't got around to watching it back yet. I'm hesitant to, in case it doesn't look as good as it felt it went.

Of course after all the focus in training on sparring I have come out of it a better fighter. I kick harder, I move better than I did before, I punch harder but looking back at it now the challenge of the nidan is more to do with the mental than the physical. Without the right mindset you won't get the discipline required to achieve the level of physical fitness needed. Without the right mindset and focus it would be difficult to get though thirty fights.

I don't feel like I need to hear the approval I thought I did. Hopefully I did a good job and that spoke for itself. As I said what I have learned though training for the nidan grading has already benefited me in my personal life. Aside from my children, it is my greatest achievement and I feel very fortunate to have had the opportunity to have undertaken it.

Mike Thornton, 2015

The Thirty Man was, for me, a way (albeit a kinda backwards way!) to pick myself up after a drawn-out period of being flat-lined in my training and in my life. It is a test that leaves you nowhere to hide, that's the real beauty of it and not just the grading on the day. All the training, conditioning, discipline up to the test – and mitigating the consequences of injuries during this time created the test within the test – to keep it up and not quit in my mind.

Feeling heavy and slow was a real issue for me and this feeling didn't leave till about two months before. Having started training nine months before the June grading, I was nearly seven months along when Sensei Gavin gave me a ladder to run footwork drills on at about the same time Sensei Goran was moving Jake and me onto sets of punch/kick combinations, combined with extra cardio exercises, ramping up our fitness and combinations. I really felt I'd turned a corner and could move the way I wanted to move for facing consecutive opponents, taking punishment and getting really tired.

With hindsight I would advise anyone taking this Thirty Man to (as well as everything else) spar, over and over and over again... with as many strong, able senior belts as they can find. When you feel like 'that's enough' go and do more sparring, with the strongest guys in the dojo and keep doing it. Injury, time, fatigue will push against you but keep doing it, regardless... because, during the final ten fights you'll never want to quit more. Then, right then, you'll remember your training, how it felt when you wanted to quit (and didn't) earlier in the year, then you'll have the guts to finish it.

Jake Hoban, 2015

My initial feeling on reaching black belt was that I would never do another grading. Not because it was so terrible, but because it was nice not to have the pressure I'd felt for the previous few years and just to be able to train for my own learning and enjoyment. And I certainly didn't consider myself in the same league as the people I had seen do the Thirty Man. But as time went on and I kept training, the Thirty Man began to creep into my head. I noticed it most in the gym, where I was focusing on heavy weights. As I psyched myself up to pick up the bar, I found myself imagining an opponent facing me, and putting on my 'war face' to steel myself for the fight. I realised that the Thirty Man was simply a part of my chosen path and there was no way round it.

Eventually I decided to broach the topic with Sensei Gavin at summer school two years after my black belt grading, only to find that he approached me first. So that was that, I was going to do the Thirty Man and I had a year to prepare. I spoke to Sempai Goran and he started giving me drills to do.

The initial drills looked nothing like anything you would see in the Thirty Man. Moving backwards and forwards while doing stylised punches in long, low stances, then moving on to kicking and punching combinations, backwards and forwards. This was kihon, or fundamentals, and I had been doing them for years in the dojo, but without the same level of individual attention, or the notion that it was directly tied to a fighting event. The logic was that while I had spirit and the ability to hit, I wasn't moving properly, and now was the time to fix that. A small improvement in footwork, and in coordinating it with striking, can translate into a big improvement in your ability to hit without getting hit (or at least not getting hit too much).

As the year went on I started training on Sundays with Goran and the other nidan candidates. We spent a surprising length of time on the basics, but it seemed to make sense. He would bring a kick-shield along so that after practising the drills we could work on hitting the shield in different ways while moving in and out. Finally, around Easter, we started to dial up the intensity, working in one-minute rounds, alternating a round hitting the pad while moving around, and a round of running or bodyweight exercises to keep up the heart rate. We peaked with a full thirty rounds the weekend before the Thirty Man.

Almost as an aside, Goran mentioned that of course the real thing would be much harder than the training but we shouldn't let that bother us. As the day got closer, I became more and more nervous. But on the day, my mood turned around and by the time I was up I felt in the zone and ready to go.

Looking back, a few things stand out. As I kept training in the dojo, I got plenty of advice from all sorts of people. I soon learned to put that to one side and concentrate on the progression I was getting from the regular training with Goran. Most of the advice was probably great, but you need to focus on how you are going to develop over time and that means following a fixed programme, not changing tack every time someone gives you a tip.

Fitness is essential, but it's also specific to the event. To get your black belt you will spend hours running up and down hills, doing push-ups, squats, burpees and more – then you do a bit of sparring at the end, but it's not the centrepiece of the grading. You need endurance spread out over a long time, with bursts of intensity. To get your nidan you have to punch, kick and move around for half an hour with a couple of breaks, so your fitness regime should replicate that. That means repeated short rounds, gradually building up the number and replicating the work/rest pattern of the Thirty Man. The best exercise is to hit the heavy bag, which gives you fitness and skill at the same time – but if you find your form going downhill you can mix it up with other exercises while sticking to the same system of rounds and rest.

The great thing about the Thirty Man is the chance to spend up to a year learning how to spar better. If you do this right, you can't fail to make improvements. But on the day, you won't look or feel anywhere near as good as you did in training. You will get hurt, you will be shocked by the ferocity of the line-up and you will feel tired sooner than you expect. Don't beat yourself up about it. You've already got the improved skills, but facing the line-up isn't really about skill after the first few fights. It's about not being afraid, not caring what they will throw at you, and not giving up. So at the end of the process you have two kinds of self-improvement, technical and psychological, both of which you should be very pleased about.

Honours List

The list of karate-ka who have completed the DKK Thirty
Man Kumite to date is as follows:

2000	Carl McKenzie
2001	Mark Salomone
	Genevieve Charles
2002	Steve Jones
	Jay Valle
	Goran Powell
2003	Karen Sheldon
	Caroline Clark
	Tim Clark
2004	Charmaigne Charles
2005	Saeed Jabbar
2006	Dominic Du Plooy
2007	Tunde Oladimeji
	Justin Taplin
	David Urquhart
	Oisin Carr
	Sonja Klug
	Michael Christian
	Brian Sharp

2008	Rob 'Smiley' Newton
	Ben Ellis

| 2009 | James Dingwall |
| | Cassandra Backus |

| 2010 | Siobhan Tierney |

2011	Dragos Voiculescu
	Steve Power
	Simon Mackown

| 2012 | Katharine Winstanley |

2013	Ragi McFadden
	Simon Clinch
	Andy Bremerkamp
	Ben Hung

2014	Elin Haug
	Juha Makinen
	Daniel Bard
	Rob Curtis
	Darren Heywood

2015	Philippa Lovegrove
	Jake Hoban
	Mike Thornton

APPENDIX 2

Training Schedules

I recommend setting a 5 day schedule as soon as you decide to do the test. Dojo sessions are the most important of all, so structure other sessions around them, something like this:

Monday:	Dojo
Tuesday:	Rest
Wednesday:	Dojo
Thursday:	Solo
Friday:	Rest
Saturday:	Solo
Sunday:	Coach/partner

Add morning sessions gradually, 3 to 5 times a week. Begin with kihon and cardio like running, skipping or shadow-boxing. Finish with dynamic stretching to limber up for the day, 15 to 30 minutes in total.

Training Formats and Drills

You're training for contact fighting, so what you do should revolve around the following – in order of importance:

- Sparring (hard and light)
- Striking (pads and heavy bag)
- Reaction drills (with a partner)
- Solo drills (shadow boxing, kihon-ido)
- Fitness (sprints, circuits, weights)

Make sure your weekly schedule has a healthy mix of the above. Don't waste time training in other sports. Channel all your energy into fight-training. With hard sparring you must be mindful of injuries. Do what you can without setting yourself back. Wear pads if it helps and don't be afraid to sit out rather than make an injury worse.

Structure solo and partner sessions in 3 parts comprised of 15 to 20 minutes each, in the following order:

1. Cardio: warm up with sharp footwork, ring-craft and partner drills
2. Impact: get explosive and aggressive on the pads and heavy bag
3. Conditioning: finish with circuits, weights and body-toughening

Use varied sessions like this rather than all cardio or all weights. This way there's more intensity to each section and you develop them together, like fighting. The shorter, more intense formats also help with faster recovery.

Footwork and Ring-craft

Footwork drills are the best way to begin solo and partner sessions. They make a good cardio warm-up and ingrain natural movement into your fight game.

Find a tennis court or football pitch, or mark out an area the size of a boxing ring. Keep your training within these boundaries to develop positional awareness.

The Skip-Punch Drill (400)

This is a great drill for controlling distance and range. Done correctly, it's quite demanding. Once you can do the whole 400 punches with good form and no rest, you know your footwork and cardio is in good shape.

Stand behind a line in fighting stance. Step forward so your front foot goes over the line (and move your back foot the same distance). Then step back behind the line (back foot moves first). Repeat using a steady skipping rhythm, forward and back, holding your fighting stance. Do 10 left and 10 right and switch without breaking rhythm. Continue this forward/back action and add a front punch, 10 x left, 10 x right. Repeat twice more, totalling

30 punches with each hand. Repeat using reverse punch, 3 x 10, left and right.

Next use a 2-punch combination, hitting lead hand first, 10 x left and 10 x right. Keep all punches straight to maximise range. Be quick but don't rush. Turn the hip and shoulder fully into the reverse punch. Complete each punch before stepping back. Don't compromise. Repeat with 3-, 4- and 5-punches combinations, 10 x left and 10 x right.

The full 400 punch drill looks like this (L left, R right):

1-punch front hand	10 L, 10 R x 3
1-punch reverse hand	10 L, 10 R x 3
2-punch combination	10 L, 10 R
3-punch combination	10 L, 10 R
4-punch combination	10 L, 10 R
5-punch combination	10 L, 10 R

Ring-craft: Palm to Palm

These ring-craft exercises should be done with a partner
to ensure good form. Later you can do them alone as part
of your shadow-boxing, while visualising an opponent at
all times.

Stand in front of one another in fighting stance, both left
foot forward, palms touching and elbows slightly bent.
One is the leader, the other is the follower. Keeping a
fighting stance at all times, the leader moves around the
area – forwards, backwards or rotating left or right. The
follower must maintain the same position opposite the
leader. If the leader changes feet, the follower must
instantly do the same.

This exercise builds the discipline of maintaining a
fighting stance while moving around. Keep one foot
forward and angle the body at 45 degrees to present less
target. The pressure on the palms should be light. Let
your feet do the work.

Once you can do this exercise for 5 minutes without
losing form, take it to the next level.

Ring-craft: Dalek Drill

Your partner walks forward at a steady pace with one arm straight like a dalek. You must evade the dalek by cutting away at 45 degrees while remaining in fighting stance. Stay in the area. The dalek tries to drive you into the corner or the side. You must avoid getting trapped and keep space behind you. Don't block the dalek's arm. Use evasive footwork to move your whole body off-line. Remember you're training to achieve a positional advantage from which to strike.

Once you can evade the dalek, practise 'luring' the dalek into the corner and cutting away just before you get there. Do this without taking your eyes off the dalek. It usually takes several weeks of practice to develop this positional awareness. Then pick up the pressure. Repeat the drill while your partner throws a steady stream of straight punches, aimed a few inches short.

Once your footwork and ring-craft is in place, add counter-attacks to your evasive skills. Go back to the dalek drill. However this time, move off-line and tap the dalek's arm aside with your front hand while throwing a reverse punch. As soon as the dalek feels the tap, he must stop. Strike again with the front hand and exit off the punch. Keep it all light and fluid – this is still a footwork drill. Make sure you use a good forward stance and a long straight punch so you can get out of range sooner.

Ring-craft: Shadow-boxing

Once you have this drill down with your partner, do it alone by shadow boxing and visualising your partner.

Be rigorous about keeping your opponent in mind at all times. Avoid turning or spinning around as if fighting a new attacker. Hold your focus on one attacker. This will be hard enough on the day so start practising now.

Try to build a stepping pattern that combines striking and evasion. When striking, drive forward using punches and knees. When evading, step away at 45 degrees rather than straight back. Build a basic rhythm of 2 evasive steps and 2 attacking steps and then get creative. If it helps, shadow-box to music. It's important to try and find a beat and a rhythm, so your movements become natural.

I don't recommend kicks. Shadow-boxing is mainly about connecting striking and movement. Kicking tends to interrupt the flow of your footwork and the bounce of your natural rhythm. Knees are easier to keep in time with your footwork and useful for dealing with low kicks, so use them instead.

Reaction Drills

These are a vital element in preparing for the Thirty Man Kumite. Start slowly and go at a pace you can manage. Work towards success. Speed up each week until the reactions come naturally. Use these 6 drills as part of your warm-up to build instant reactions to key attacks:

1. Front Kick Slip

Partner throws a front kick. Slip offline by moving forwards at 45 degrees and parry the kick. Strike the body with 2 punches and move away. Repeat 5 times each side for one minute.

2. Round Kick Blend

Both stand left foot forward. Your partner throws a right roundhouse to the midsection. Catch it in an over-hook while stepping around with the kick, switching stance as you do. Try and blend with the kick. As you plant your feet, strike your partner's body with the other hand. Both should now be right foot forward. Repeat on the other side. Continue left and right for one minute.

3. Low Kick Block

Your partner throws a low kick. Block with the shin and responds with 2 punches, reverse and front, before throwing a low kick of your own. Partner also blocks and throws 2 punches, creating a flow drill. Do 10 each side and change stance. Continue for one minute.

Note: all movements alternate between left and right, so a left block is followed by a right punch, then a left punch, then a right kick. This keeps momentum flowing across the shoulders and hips.

4. Low Kick Strike

Your partner throws a low kick to your front leg. Take away the target by using your front leg to throw a kick to the inside of his supporting leg. This is followed by two punches (reverse then front) and a low kick of your own. Repeat 10 times and then switch stance. Continue for one minute. This drill is better than blocking because instead of clashing shins, you disrupt his kick and land one of your own.

5. Low Kick Step

Your partner throws a low kick and steps forward. Step back to evade and then forward, throwing a low kick of your own. Replace the kicking foot behind and punch twice to the body, front hand, then reverse. This maintains the switching momentum from side to side. Another good drill because there's no clashing.

6. Tapping Hands

This is a similar to the palm-to-palm drill. Standing within striking range, your partner throws light punches to the body while you tap the top of his hands. Partner varies the punches, throwing singles and combinations. The purpose of this exercise is building alertness and reading attacks. Keep punches and taps light and work on being fast and smooth.

Grip and Clinch Drills

Getting gripped can be very damaging because your opponent tends to strike the same place over and over again and it's hard to defend. These three drills cover three ways of dealing with grips and clinches. The first and best way is to avoid them in the first place. The second is to escape once they're on. The third is to get comfortable in the clinch so instead of freezing, you take the initiative and exert some control until you can break free. Practise these three drills as a warm-down after pad-work and conditioning, using a feeling of kakie (sticking hands) to develop strength and sensitivity.

1. Grip Evasion

Rule number one for avoiding grabs is not to use them yourself. The fighters in the line take subliminal signals from the way you fight and reflect your style to some extent. If you fight nice and tidy, so do they. If you start gripping up and thrashing around, you give them the idea of doing the same, and they're fresher than you.

To practise grip evasion, have your partner walk towards you with both arms out like a zombie. Using mawashi-uke (wheeling block) and torag-uchi (two-handed push) to redirect both his arms to one side and push away.

Move around and work both sides. Once you get this working, stay closer and use minimal movement to make it more challenging. Build power by using the Sanchin posture and heavy, sticking hands.

Next, allow yourself to be gripped and work on circling limb movements and evasive footwork to break free. Make it more real by wearing a gi-top. Try to break the grip early before it's on tight.

2. Thai Clinch Escape

Knee strikes are among the most devastating of all attacks. They can easily break ribs and if your head's down, you risk getting hit in the face. In general, keep your head up and your posture straight so your opponent can't drag you forward.

Begin by having your partner clasp his hands behind your

head in the Thai clinch. Stand close and use Sanchin posture to avoid getting bent forward. Meanwhile work on freeing yourself by feeding your arms through his and driving his head back with your forearm. Start lightly and increase resistance gradually.

Next, get your partner to pull your head down and throw 3 knee strikes. Block these with your forearms using an X-shaped block, keeping the arms extended and using some 'give'. Don't clasp your forearms on your body or they'll break. Redirect the third knee-strike to the side, lift under the thigh and throw. Alternatively, follow the third knee down (this is the safest time to move) and pop your head out to the side, using mawashi-uke to clear the arms.

3. Clinch Control

The big danger with being gripped is freezing and running out of ideas. When this happens you can eat a lot of unanswered blows. If you can learn to feel comfortable in the clinch you can prevent a lot of attacks and even get a bit of a rest, like a boxer clinching up for a breather. The key is to stay proactive and initiate movement, forcing your opponent to react instead of giving him control.

Begin by doing the pummel drill for a minute to get a sense of body-to-body engagement. Then clinch up and move around, taking it in turns to lift the other person off the ground using a variety of lifts. This helps to develop balance and control. Start playfully and get used to the movements. Then work on blocking the lifts, turn for turn. Use Sanchin posture so your whole body feels engaged.

Still in the clinch, have your partner throw some slow low kicks. Disrupt the kicks by jamming the shoulder on the kicking side, or by pulling his head forward to disrupt his balance. This takes the sting out of a kick even if it lands.

Finish by sparring from the clinch, working on controlling and disrupting your opponent's posture and checking attacks at the hip or shoulder. Learn to conserve energy and wait for the break, so you can get back to your basic strategy of hit and move.

Kihon-ido

Moving basics is a great way to build and hone the fundamentals of good kumite. I still use it in my own training as routine maintenance for power, balance and natural momentum. Working in zenkutsu dachi (front stance) helps to develop power through your full range of motion and throw bodyweight into punches, even if you're moving backwards. This is a vital aspect of controlling distance.

I recommend kihon-ido in the morning as a great way to get your vital energy flowing. Start relaxed and keep the movements smooth, long and powerful. Try to feel the natural swing of momentum across the shoulders and hips as the techniques flow from one to the next. As you warm up, speed up and add power and focus. Always use a long stance and full range of motion.

Some fighters already have great basics and there's no need to spend a lot of time on it. However if your fighting is a little scrappy and you struggle to land clean techniques, this is usually reflected in less-than-perfect basics. Rest assured, any time invested in kihon-ido is never wasted. The exercises should be quite basic, working in zenkutsu dachi and using straight punches and simple combinations. Check your stances and positions in the mirror and video yourself from time to time. Better still, get a senior grade to correct your technique. The aim is to do simple techniques perfectly. Long stances, clean lines, strong focus. The benefits of this will seep into everything else you do.

5x5 Kihon-Ido

This routine covers the fundamentals of kumite: punching using full range, maintaining rotational momentum and managing low kicks. All stances are zenkutsu dachi (front stance) unless otherwise specified.

1. Step forward and throw 5 straight punches to the midsection – 5 x forwards and 5 x back.

2. Step forward lower block, reverse punch, pull back into neko ashi dachi (cat stance) with lower block, drive forward into zenkutsu dachi with reverse punch, front punch – 5 x forwards and 5 x back.

3. Raise the front knee in a shin block. Step forward front kick. Land in zenkutsu dachi and throw 3 punches: reverse, front, reverse – 5 x forwards.
Going back: step back with lower block. Front kick off the back leg and replace the leg behind. Throw 3 punches: front, reverse, front – 5 x back.

4. Raise the front foot in a shin block and replace it where it was. Throw 2 punches, reverse and front. Step forward with a low kick and reverse punch – 5 x forwards.
Going back: step back into zenkutsu dachi and low kick off the front leg. Reverse punch and front punch. Raise the front knee in a shin block and replace the foot where it was, finish with reverse punch – 5 x back.

5. Low kick off the front leg and replace the foot where it was. Throw 2 punches: reverse and front. Step forward with a low kick and reverse punch – 5 x forwards.
Going back: low kick off the front foot and place it back behind you (this is tricky and requires good balance).

Throw 2 punches: front then reverse. Low kick off the front foot and replace where it was, then reverse punch – 5 x back.

Striking: Bag and Pads

If you're training alone, try to use a full-length heavy bag so you can work low kicks as well as body shots. If you have a partner, using a kick-shield is more like hitting the body than Thai pads, and better for low kicks.

Before beginning your strike-training, it's important to get into the right frame of mind. You must be alert and aggressive. If you stand still in front of the bag, hit softly and take rests, you're training dangerous habits. Better not to strike at all and come back when you're up for it. (That's not to say you can't warm up, especially if the bag is heavy and cold. Begin lightly and build up to full power before beginning your programme.)

The key to smart bag-work is controlling distance at all times. Drill this by repeating the skip-punch drill on the bag to begin your session. This is 6 one-minute rounds of straight punching, starting with singles (front and reverse) and then 2, 3, 4 and 5-punch combinations. Each combination has a step in and out. This takes some doing but persevere until you can do six rounds with speed and power.

Once you have the first six rounds down, work one-minute rounds of front kicks, low kicks, round-kicks and hooks and uppercuts to the body. Take another 2 minute rest.

Finish with 3 one-minute rounds of combinations of your choice, making sure to step in and out with each one. If you have a pad-holder, they can move a step or two between each combination to ensure you use footwork and ring-craft.

Fitness: Sprints

Running, and especially sprints, is the best cardio for fight training. The pumping action of the arms and legs has some similarity to punching, making it a better approximation than other cardio like cycling and rowing. If you have injuries that prevent normal running, the Nordic skier is a good alternative with a similar pumping action.

Think of cardio as a supplement to your regular training – a way to push your existing fitness to new heights. Remember running itself is not the aim.

Sprints are ideal because they build power and work quickly. A few minutes of sprints can tire you as much as a three mile run, but you recover faster and there's less stress on your joints from pounding the road.

Level sprints on a track or field work slightly differently to hill sprints, but both are good. Level sprints build speed and grace, while hill sprints build raw grunt and power.

Based on my rule of training what you're not good at, work on what you lack most. If you're naturally light and fast, build strength with hill sprints. If you're slow and strong, build speed with level sprints.

If you're a keen runner and like to do longer distances of 3 to 5 miles that's okay, but don't overdo it. Make sure your runs aren't eating into the energy you need for dojo training, partner-work and bag-work, which are more important.

Conditioning: circuits & weights

Like running, conditioning should be seen as a supplement to core training, not a replacement. Add conditioning exercises in the final third of your training sessions, after your skill-drills and your bag or pad-work is done.

Work in one-minute bursts against constantly changing resistance. This can be bodyweight, weights, or both. Move smoothly from one exercise to the next so you're always working. Use whole-body exercises as much as possible. Plyometrics are good for kick-starting a killer workout but hard to maintain throughout. (Plyometrics use jumping or bouncing to build explosive power.)

If you're outdoors and there are no weights available, here are some sample circuits designed to work The Big Four (legs, chest, abs and back):

1. Jump squats
2. Take-off push-ups

3. Squat thrusts
4. Dorsal raises with 4 punches

1. Lunges
2. Knuckle push-ups
3. Sit-ups
4. Bridge

Don't worry too much about how many you do, just keep going with each exercise until you lose form and switch to the next. Keep working for one minute. Rest 20 seconds and repeat.

Some exercises like burpees work several areas at once. Make them jumping burpees and add a push-up to build more power. Burpees integrate well with cardio exercises like sprints or shadow-boxing, for example:

1. Sprint across a football pitch
2. 5 x jumping burpees with a push-up
3. Sprint back
4. 5 x jumping burpees with a push-up

Or: 10 jumping burpees with a push-up followed by 30 seconds of shadow boxing

If you're training at a gym, use weights in your circuit. I like barbells with set weights of around 25, 35 and 45 kg for men (less for women) so you don't have to lose time by changing weights.

Use one-minute rounds working against continuous resistance. This builds good cardio and power endurance. Intersperse each barbell set with something like push-ups, dips, chins or sit-ups. (I'm not a fan of bench press for fight training because it's a little too sedentary).

- With the lighter bar, work on cleans, lunges, shoulder press and bent-over rows
- With the medium bar do deep squats, shoulder press, bent-over rows and deadlifts
- With the heavier bar concentrate on squats and deadlifts, you might only manage one or two of the other exercises

Use gym sessions to build a strong back, which is hard to do outside. Squats, deadlifts and bent-over rows are all good for this. Keep your abs engaged and work your core.

Conditioning: Body-toughening

Use body-toughening exercises carefully. Begin gently and build up over time. Do them towards the end of sessions otherwise they deaden the limbs and make the rest of your training difficult. Train them at the same time as conditioning exercises to make sure the torso and limbs are pumped and warm. The main purpose of these exercises is not to deaden the flesh and bones but rather to teach you to make subtle adjustments in muscular tension and breathing. This allows you to take powerful strikes without undue concern.

Step forwards in a fighting stance and breathe out, tensing the torso and legs using 'Sanchin'. Have your partner throw a 4-part combination to your body or legs with medium power. Watch where the strikes are landing. Tense the area of impact and exhale in time with the strikes. Step forward and repeat 10 times. Your partner or coach must work towards success, not failure, so build up the power each week. Remember you need to train again tomorrow.

The Last Eight Weeks

In the last eight weeks the focus is no longer on perfecting technique but rather on pushing what you've got to the max. Structure your training to create a steady progression from 15 one-minute rounds in the first week to 30 by the last week.

Begin each session with footwork and reaction drills to warm up. By now these should be tidy, crisp and sharp. If they're too easy, combine two or even three drills to add complexity and intensity.

Once you're fully warmed-up, take a minute to walk along your imaginary line-up and call out the names of the fighters you see. This drops adrenaline and charges you up, ready to go.

Hit some hard sprints and then go straight into one-minute rounds. Do sets of 7 : 5 : 3 rounds with a 2 minute break between sets. This is roughly the pace you're going to be working at over the next eight weeks, however you're going to extend the numbers a little each week.

Keep the first 7 rounds focused mainly on straight punches and sharp footwork moving around the area. Then take a 2 minute break and walk along your imaginary line. Hit a couple of sprints and then go into 5 one-minute rounds of kicks, hooks and uppercuts. Take another 2 minute break and walk the line. Call out the names of fighters. Do 3 rounds to finish consisting of 30 seconds on the pads, 5 burpees and 5 body-toughening combinations.

If your form dips or flags too low, stop and warm down. If you're still operating at high revs with good form, add a couple of rounds next week. Once you get good, step up the intensity by throwing in extra sprints between rounds.

In the first four weeks, don't be in a hurry to add rounds. Add intensity. Around week 4 or 5 there is often a slump week due to the increased pressure of training. Give yourself an extra couple of days to recover and come back fresh so you can hit a new plateau.

Over the 8 week course your sets of one-minute rounds should look something like this:

7 : 5 : 3
7 : 5 : 5
8 : 6 : 6
10 : 8 : 6
10 : 8 : 6 (slump week, no improvement)
10 : 8 : 8
10 : 10 : 8
10 : 10 : 10

Naturally you can structure your progress to suit you, but be sure to build on intensity rather than training long and slow.

The Final Week

Your last hard session should be one week before the test. You'll probably want to do 10 : 10 : 10 rounds to give yourself confidence, so go ahead. It'll feel hard, and in my experience, it isn't always your best session. The accumulated effect of intense training over eight weeks will make you feel jaded, so don't worry if it's a bit of a grind. All the more reason for the next part of your training – a difficult part, as it happens – which is to relax.

Easier said than done, but be strong and force yourself to do it. Go to the cinema. Spend time with the family. Sit home watching box-sets in your onesie. Read up on Goju Ryu karate, because there will be questions as part of your grading. If you want to keep moving, run through your kata gently to make sure you can remember it. After a few days your body will want to train, missing the high of the endorphins. After a few more days, it'll be screaming to train hard. Ignore it. There are two full days of training before the line-up, so you'll be glad of the freshness and there'll be no danger of going in cold.

If negative thoughts start to invade your mind, balance them out with positive ones. Think beyond the test to the moment of completion, the honour of the nidan certificate, the moment you wrap the black gi around you, the evening by the campfire when you bask in glory. Maybe. The taste of that first beer. Definitely. The chance to put all this pressure behind you and return to a normal life. Perhaps… because many nidans secretly admit to missing the singular focus of the test once it's gone. Everyday life can seem quite ordinary without it.

After fifteen years of involvement in Thirty Man Kumite, I know one thing for certain: we each get the test we deserve. Whatever work we've done is done. Every hard session is in the bank. Every morning you got up early is logged. Every blow you took in training in registered. Don't think too much more about it. Ultimately the Thirty Man Kumite is a leap of faith, so just trust in your training… and jump.

Acknowledgements

I'd like to thank the candidates who trusted me to coach them and worked so hard in our training: Charmaigne, Dominic Du Plooy, Siobhan Tierney, Dragos Voiculescu, Ben Hung, Ragi McFadden, Daniel Bard, Juha Makinen, Jake Hoban, Mike Thornton, and Laila Al-Minawi and Ed Barbor who are training with me this year. Thank you too to Simon Clinch and the fighters from DKK Bristol who added their valuable insights: Simon Mackown, Katharine Winstanley, Andy Bremerkamp, Rob Curtis, Darren Heywood and Philippa Lovegrove.

I must acknowledge DKK's chief instructors Gavin Mulholland and Dan Lewis who've made this epic test possible year after year. Since my first summer camp in 2000 they've enabled so many martial artists to reach this pinnacle in karate training. A personal achievement like the Thirty Man Kumite is for many without equal. It's a testament to the instruction and personal qualities of our teachers that students return year after year, taking the standard ever higher in this small but incredibly tight-knit brotherhood.

Finally I'd like to thank those who helped me whip this text into shape, including, again, Gavin Mulholland, my father Michael, Jake Hoban, Mike Thornton and Frances Little, and Ben Hung for his insight and patience with the cover design.

BOOKS BY
GORAN POWELL

Waking Dragons

The Thirty Man Kumite is one of karate's toughest tests, reserved for senior black belts with years of experience. One person fights a line-up of thirty fighters, one after another, full contact, moving up the grades to face the strongest, most dangerous fighters last.

Waking Dragons is a true account of Goran Powell's Thirty Man Kumite and the lifetime of martial arts that led up to it. He covers the fitness training and mental preparations required for such a brutal test, talking openly of the conquest of fear and the spiritual growth that is at the heart of the traditional martial arts.

One of those rare books that you want to keep reading because it's so good, but fear reaching the end because then it will be over
Waterstones

Quite simply, this book is impossible to put down
Traditional Karate Magazine

An exciting and tense read with lots of action
Martial Arts Magazine

The author's journey is one in which we can find great wisdom, information that all martial artists should know
Lawrence Kane

It inspired me, and I know it will inspire you
Geoff Thompson

Shines a light into the darkest reaches of your psyche
Graham Wendes

While he relays the fight sequences in almost terrifyingly brutal detail, what really hits you is the real battles are won and lost in the mind
Doug Wood

Chojun – a novel

A typhoon brings the renowned karate master Chojun Miyagi into the life of young Kenichi Ota, who must prove himself before he can enter the master's inner circle. As once-peaceful Okinawa prepares for war, master and student venture to China in search of the deepest meaning of karate.

After Pearl Harbour, the tides of war turn against Japan and an American invasion fleet approaches. Kenichi is conscripted as a runner for the Japanese general staff and finds himself in the epicentre of the Battle of Okinawa. In the aftermath, he must fight again to rebuild the shattered hopes of his people and preserve his master's art.

Riveting, highly recommended – Lawrence Kane

Remarkable, it's that good! – Kris Wilder

Goran Powell has a marvellous way of capturing the tone of Asian storytelling – Loren W Christensen

Covers the relationship between student and Sensei beautifully – Nick Hughes

An exciting step in the evolution of how karate's history is told – Mike Clarke

Detailed, meticulously researched and absolutely compelling – Geoff Thompson

Enthralling… hard to put down – Violet Li

AWARDS

Winner: Eric Hoffer Award
Silver: Benjamin Franklin, Historical Fiction
Bronze: eLit Awards
Finalist: Book of the Year, ForeWord Magazine
Finalist: International Book Award

A Sudden Dawn – fiction

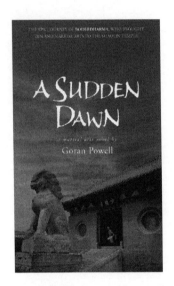

The life of Bodhidharma is steeped in myth and legend, 'A Sudden Dawn' is one version of his story. Born to the warrior caste, Bodhidharma gives up a glorious future as a soldier to become a monk and seek enlightenment. After years of searching in vain, he becomes enlightened in a single moment.

He accepts a mission to travel to China and spread the Buddha's teachings. On the way he meets an unlikely disciple, a Chinese fugitive named Ko. Together they venture to the Emperor's palace in Nanjing and beyond, to a temple in the mountains, Shaolin. But there are powerful forces at work to destroy the Indian master, and Ko's violent past catches up with him at the temple gate where a deadly reckoning must take place.

The book martial artists have been waiting 2000 years for Chris Crudelli, Mind Body & Kickass Moves

Bridges the gap between training and spirituality. Fabulously entertaining – Combat Magazine

Destined to become an epic tale of the warrior's journey
Patrick McCarthy

Inspirational, beautifully written, I loved it
Geoff Thompson

Weaves fact and fiction to produce a powerhouse of a page turner – Iain Abernethy

You can feel the hot breath of battle on your neck and the cool of the temple's damp hallways on your legs
Kris Wilder

As good as James Clavell's 'Shogun' – Lawrence Kane

Superbly crafted characters, surges with action
Loren W. Christensen

Walk alongside one of mankind's greatest legends
Gavin Mulholland

Awards

Winner: USA Book News, Historical Fiction 2010
Gold: eLit 2011, Gold: IP LivingNow 2011

Matryoshka – Cold War Thriller

The deadly arts of Soviet special forces are not lost, they have simply adapted to the new world order. Eva was once a soldier of the Cold War, trained in seduction and espionage, known as a 'Matryoshka' (Russian Doll). Today she is an art dealer in London but beneath the outer shell the Matryoshka is still at work.

When an operation goes wrong she is traced by a ghost from her past, her instructor Vasili Dimitriev. Dimitriev is hunting a traitor in Moscow. But the traitor has sent an Alpha team to silence both of them. As British police and the CIA close in, Eva and Vasili must work together in the deadliest game of all, where trust is weakness and love is a weapon.

Spies, Soviets, London...fighting! Treat yourself, you will enjoy – Kris Wilder

The author's knowledge of combat skills shines through Gary Chamberlain

I can't help feeling Goran must have lived (impossible) in all the cities and times he sets Matryoshka in to bring them to life the way he does Stuart Williams

The author's intimate understanding of combat makes the scenes so vivid, it's like watching a Hollywood action movie – Simon Clinch

The depth and intrigue of Homeland, and set with a Cold War background – Tim Clark

An engrossing action thriller from cover to cover, I couldn't put it down – Mike Thornton

About the Author

Goran Powell is an award-winning freelance writer and martial artist who holds a 5th dan in Goju Ryu Karate. He works in London and teaches and trains at Daigaku Karate Kai, one of the UK's strongest clubs.

For more visit **goranpowell.com**

22383742R00127

Printed in Great Britain
by Amazon